For more information, address:
sandytermotto@gmail.com

ISBN: 978-0-9850359-8-3
First printing, 2021

1944—PRESENT

SIX LIVES OF A BROOKLYN BOY

A JOURNEY DEALING WITH HONESTY, INTEGRITY, PRINCIPLES, AND COMMITMENT

BY SANDY S. TERMOTTO

TABLE OF CONTENTS

PROLOGUE

In writing this book, I took the liberty of assuming a lighter approach to my life experiences, perhaps seeking to elicit a smile in spite of the gravity of the circumstances.

I am writing from memory and possibly, sometimes vicariously. I changed a few names and omitted some people out of respect for their privacy and comfort.

I have written this book to allow my descendants to have knowledge of the events in my life and their heritage.

Keywords Covering My Philosophy of Life:
Honesty
Integrity
Principles
Commitment

ACKNOWLEDGMENTS

Linda Termotto

Joseph Valenti

Kristen Singagliese

Dave Shealy

Ashley Johnson, Editor

1
A BROOKLYN BOY

I was born in Tampa, Florida, on May 10, 1944. My father was a staff sergeant stationed at MacDill Army Airfield. My parents lived in the carriage house of Dr. Frank Adamo, a Japanese prisoner of war and a heroic survivor of the Bataan Death March. Dr. Adamo is memorialized by a Tampa highway named in his honor.

Since all of our family lived in New York City, my grandmother and Uncle Phil came to Tampa to assist my mother. During this time, a strong friendship between my maternal grandfather, Onofrio Modica, and the Santo Trafficante family was reestablished. Both families came from the same area of Sicily, and today my closest friend, Dr. Joseph Valenti, who I met in Vietnam, is from Tampa.

78th Street

I grew up living at 1749 78th Street in Brooklyn, New York, in a two-family home owned by my grandfather Termotto. We lived on the ground floor. My family consisted of my mother, Martha, and my father, Arthur; my brother, Nolan; and my sister, Catherine, nicknamed "The Brat," because she was the youngest and frequently teased. My father, often called "Red" for his reddish-brown hair, was an athletic 6-foot, 200-pound man. My Brooklyn-raised mother graduated with honors from the all-girls Bay Ridge High School.

The second floor was home to my Aunt Rose, Uncle Joseph Russo, and four cousins: Frankie, Nolan, Joey, and Philip. My maternal grandparents lived within walking distance. My mother, one of nine children, grew up there with her large family: two boys and seven girls. My grandparents on my father's side had six children: one girl and five boys. Thus, we had a familial bond in our immediate neighborhood.

Our activities were home-oriented most of the time but usually included various ballgames whenever space permitted. We used the streets, sidewalks, and schoolyards; our games were named by the area: square, triangle, and stoopball. If you didn't grow up on the streets of Brooklyn, you probably wouldn't recognize our games that had fluid rules to fit the space in which we had to play. You would also be unfamiliar with playing football, baseball, or stickball on concrete since grass fields were very rare. Lamp posts or manhole covers were designated as foul lines or home run distances.

To give my mother and Aunt Rose a break from caring for the kids, our fathers would occasionally take us to Prospect Park to ride horses. While we rode horses, my father was betting on them. These moments—early hints of my father's gambling problem—were also among my first experiences with horseback riding. I had no idea the role these two would play in the coming years.

In our household, every night at 9 p.m. one of us had to run to the corner store to get the "number" for the day. This ritual reflected the amount of cash bet at the racetrack the day before. There was also "the sheet," which listed the horses entered to race the following afternoon at various racetracks. Some people in our neighborhood were so addicted to gambling that they would bet on the first digit of the license plate of the next car to make a right-hand turn. Unfortunately, this obsession with gambling resulted in the loss of homes and many divorces.

I remember my parents discussing financial concerns related

to my father's gambling. The community I grew up in involved daily gambling by betting on horse races and playing the numbers and high stakes card games. Having witnessed this first-hand, I never bet on anything significant.

Bensonhurst

The experience of living in Bensonhurst, a primarily Sicilian section of Brooklyn, was a mixture of Italian food, music, and occasional comedy. From street corner doo-wop singing groups and rock-and-roll bands to Italian tenors and opera, it all came together in the ethnic pulse of Brooklyn.

Recreation centered around activities for fun and sport. No one even thought about taking drugs to get high. Our highs came from our family, our culture, and our friends. Discipline and respect for people and property fortified this way of life.

Living in Bensonhurst, we frequently identified our acquaintances with a characteristic that captured the essence of their persona. Some of these nicknames were:

Joe Birds: had a pigeon coop on his roof and bred racing and carrier pigeons

Junior da, da, da, da: had a severe stuttering problem

Vinny Doo Doo: frequently had to use the bathroom

Paulie the Pope: a widely respected man

Big Junior: a huge guy named after his small father

Sally the Sheik: a very well-groomed and sharp dresser

Willie Monster: over 6-foot tall and big

Jerry Black: exceptionally dark skin and hair

Jimmie the Blonde: few fair-haired people in the neighborhood

Jimmy Blue Eyes: unusual to see someone in the mostly Sicilian neighborhood with blue eyes

Jimmy the Gimp: walked funny due to neurological damage

Jimmy Coca Cola: wore very thick lenses in his eyeglasses

Lou the Tailor: learned to make clothes from his father

Johnny Knock Knock: owner of a widely known bar, the Knock-Knock Inn

Joe TV: the only neighborhood repairman in the early days of black-and-white television

Spike Shoes: loved baseball and frequently wore his baseball cleats on and off the field

Aurelio: the "golden one" in Italian; he had a likable personality

Louie the Con: arrested and convicted several times

Punchy: an amateur boxer in the neighborhood

Dynamite Joe: volatile and got into trouble

Sandy Arms: arms that were significantly larger than normal from weight lifting

Sammy the Bull: very strong, tough individual

Fat Eddy: very pleasant but grossly overweight

Frankie Bugs: was not "right" mentally

Crazy Angelo: mentally ill and constantly walked circles around the block

Fo-Fo: someone who tended to menial tasks such as a lookout for undercover detectives

Cretino: a dumb person

Inga Dinga: nickname for a man who was "mixed up;" for example, Jimmy, Inga Dinga!

Many members of organized crime families resided in this

community, making it a very low crime area. The watchful eyes of the enclave maintained safety. It was rumored that St. Bernadette's church and parish played a major role in laundering money through the olive oil industry for some significant families.

My grandfather Modica owned a bakery in Bensonhurst. In addition to the large bakery, my grandparents owned several adjacent structures, one of which was a men's social club that brought together people for discussion of events and business "dealings." Beneath the bakery and club was a wine cellar that housed the family wines, grape presses, and oak-aging casks. Producing quality wine for family and friends was a great source of pride.

Eventually, other structures were built, including a shrine to Saint Anthony, the patron saint of lost and stolen articles. Many people gave alms in thanksgiving to God for his blessings. The shrine, on 81st Street near 17th Avenue, became a very revered area in Bensonhurst, and locals would stop and offer prayers for the poor and needy.

St. Anthony's life symbolizes what every Christian's life should be: steady courage to face the ups and downs encountered. It is the call to love and forgive, to be concerned with the needs of others, and to have our feet solidly on the ground.

Bensonhurst Weddings

Growing up, I remember attending the wedding ceremonies of friends and family members. By and large, Micali Terrace, formerly a bowling alley, catered many of the classic wedding receptions. My most outstanding memory about the food was that they gave you *so much* heaped onto family-size tables. The quantity was of utmost importance. The location of sandwiches led this type of wedding to be called a "football wedding." If you wanted a meatball sandwich at one end of the table, the response would be "Here, catch this!" as someone tossed a wrapped sandwich across to you. Big Vinnie and the House Rockers was the usual band. At the end of the meal, the lights were dimmed for the flaming cherries jubilee—complete with sparklers for effect. With all the eating, conversing, and singing, people did not notice that the dance floor consisted of the wooden lane markers from a previous bowling alley.

Next came a loud drum roll to summon the bride and groom up to the bandstand. Frankie and Johnnie Micali spoke at length to the bride and groom about family, children, and God's love. At this time, with the bride and groom anxious to leave, a special gift was unveiled: a four-foot-tall statue of Saint Anthony for them to carry home. Finally, they were able to proceed with their honeymoon.

At the other end of the spectrum were the more sophisticated, upscale wedding receptions. The wedding reception venues were very fancy, featuring the best of everything. Many of the guests arrived via taxicab because they did not want to have their license plates noted by the FBI who were surveilling the building. The taxi drivers did not realize their passengers might have been wearing $3,000 suits with cashmere and vicuna overcoats. The drivers understood to keep their mouths shut and not provide any information to the FBI.

As the guests entered the reception hall for the cocktail hour, the men would congregate and drift off to one side of the room and the women to the other. There was a lot of hugging and kissing to show respect between the men who had not seen each other recently. The menu for the cocktail hour primarily consisted of lobster, lamb chops, and other delicious foods that could have sufficed as a main meal in itself.

As the newly wedded couple was introduced, they would rise out of the floor on a glass pedestal. Once the cocktail hour was over, everyone moved to the ballroom for the main course, which included a choice of entrées.

After leisurely dining, dancing, and conversing, the next phase of the celebration began in "The Viennese" room. In this room, sumptuous desserts, including various cheeses, fruits, nuts, and after-dinner beverages, were served. Italian pastries and biscotti were also offered. The famous line from the movie *The Godfather* could be heard throughout the room, "Don't Forget the Cannolis!" Prior to departing, guests received wedding favors and a bag of Brooklyn bagels. These memorable affairs lasted about six hours.

Grandfather Onofrio Modica and The Bakery

Grandfather Modica enjoyed having family dinners, and he sat at the head of the table with a jug of wine within easy reach. By the end of a leisurely multicourse dinner, everyone was enjoying themselves.

Grandpa loved Grandma, and after the family meal, he would frequently get on one knee and recite spontaneous poetry to her. They had raised nine children and yet always showed affection toward each other. Dinner was usually followed by my cousin Frank and me taking out our guitars and playing Italian songs such as "Come Back to Sorrento," "O'Solo Mio," and "Malefemena."

In the beginning, author's
grandparents and family

Grandmother and Grandfather
Modica with their nine children at
their 50th wedding anniversary

Even though my grandparents had a full-time nanny, raising so many children was no easy task. Nellie was the housekeeper, and she functioned as one of the family. Observing the logistics involved, my grandfather had the foresight to buy a house in the country. After school was out, my grandmother, Nellie, and the children were transported two and a half hours to the country house situated along the pristine Musconetcong River in New Hampton, New Jersey. Thus, all of the children had the opportunity to enjoy living away from the steamy, congested city.

As the number of grandchildren increased, schedules were arranged so everyone got a vacation. Most of the country activity involved walking to the Changewater General Store and swimming in the river. Fishing was a regular fair-weather occurrence.

On one very successful fishing day, I felt nature's calling. I quickly handed over my rod and reel to my Uncle Lou, who was there merely observing for safety reasons. I hadn't left for more than five minutes when a game warden showed up and requested to see my Uncle Lou's fishing license. My uncle explained that he was just holding my rod and bucket while I went to the bathroom; however, he received a summons for fishing without a license. The "city slickers" learned the hard way.

As a youngster, I spent many hours working in my grandfather's bakery, Modica's Bakery, observing his demeanor. Countless people in this Italian community would thank him for helping them in their time of need. Often, he asked for nothing in return. He understood from dealing with people that their character, principles, and values were reflected in performance. My grandfather was a quiet, powerful, and understated man with a low profile. His word was his bond, sealed with a handshake, not a 20-page contract. He was an extremely patriotic man. On election day, he would dress up in his finest clothes and go to vote with his friends and family.

As the nine children grew up, they rotated working schedules in the bakery since it was operational almost 24 hours a day. Three separate coal-fired brick ovens kept bread and cookies fresh all the time. Delivery vehicles transported baked goods to various neighborhood grocery stores and school cafeterias. The bakery was always bustling and, during the holidays, made special types of bread and cookies.

For Italians, Christmas Eve typically features seven types of seafood before midnight and meat, such as sausage, afterward. Thanksgiving, of course, featured turkey. As a service to his many customers, my grandfather Modica tagged their turkeys with numbers and roasted them in his brick ovens. One time, the mischievous grandkids, myself included, decided to have some "fun" by switching the identifying number tags. Upon picking up their turkeys, pandemonium ensued. The turkeys and pans did not match up with the customers' numbered tags. After the panic subsided, everyone received the correct turkey and pan. I can still remember my grandfather shaking his head, saying, "Inutile–" which translated to "These kids are useless–."

On cold winter nights, after working in the bakery, my cousins and I would stash hot loaves of bread in our jackets, close to our chests, to keep us warm on our walk home. On occasion, since I did not own an automobile, I would use the bread truck to pick up a date. I can still smell the aroma of pignoli cookies, sesame cookies, and biscotti anisette.

A Note Regarding Grandpa Termotto

My paternal grandfather, Saverio Termotto, was a skilled concrete mason employed in the construction of the Empire State Building up to the 86th floor. I am very proud to know that he contributed his expertise in building this landmark. His love for his adopted country was unmatched. Unfortunately, my grandmother, Caterina, succumbed to a stroke in her early years, leaving five sons and one daughter. Despite this heartbreak, he persevered, providing love and support for his children: Arthur, Benjamin, Anthony, Joseph, John, and Jean. In February 1945, his son John was killed in a military air training accident.

After an extended period of mourning, Grandpa Termotto requested his children's opinion regarding the possibility of marriage for companionship. All approved. Grandpa married "Aunt Katie," who was a widow. Unfortunately, three of Grandpa's four remaining sons died before they were 64 years old. He found solace in his vegetable garden and tended to his fig tree. I don't think he ever overcame the loss of his wife and children. Very little else was known of Grandpa Termotto's life.

Guiding Life Principles

Early recognition of the love of family has remained with me until today. My early experiences have given me a solid foundation for dealing with life. Four words that, inspired by my early memories, have positively influenced me through the years are *honesty, integrity, principles, and commitment.*

Proud patriot Grandfather Termotto and his five sons

2

LESSONS IN MUSIC AND LIFE

G rowing up in the Bensonhurst neighborhood of Brooklyn was a major influence on music in my life. It stimulated me mentally, technically, socially, and financially.

When I was 11 years old, my parents renovated our basement. This became a place for cousins and friends to congregate. The finished basement served, for a while, as a hub for study activity, but eventually it became a rehearsal studio for local music groups.

During the 1950s and '60s, it was common for neighborhood singers to congregate on street corners, bringing aspiring vocalists and musical groups together. The use of my home basement as a rehearsal studio was convenient. However, the narrow

The author working with the Passions

alleyway between the Loew's Oriental Theatre and Kelly's Pool Room in Brooklyn had the best sound quality. Both had high brick walls and produced resonant echoes. Two well-known vocal groups evolved from this alley: the Mystics, who had a #2 hit with "Hush-a-Bye," and the Passions, who had a hit with "Just to Be With You." Multiple groups recorded albums that included the song "Searching for the Echo."

During this time, music became a significant force in my life. This was the era of Elvis Presley, Les Paul, Andres Segovia, and rock-and-roll. Playing the guitar was the goal of many youngsters since it was an easily transported, very social instrument suitable for a broad spectrum of musical styles.

On occasion, the "boys" that hung out in the White Rock Bar on the corner of my street would call me and my cousin Frankie to play some songs for them. They often insisted that we accept a few dollars to show their gratitude. Rock-and-roll music was very popular with teenagers, but I learned the value of studying the classics early on. Once you studied and understood them, you would then be able to play a broad spectrum of music, not just simple rock-and-roll strumming.

At get-togethers, my grandfather Modica and family would sing traditional Italian songs. My parents often requested songs from the 1920s, '30s, and '40s. Included in my repertoire were blues and country selections. By playing all genres, I began to understand how music would open up an entirely new world for me. I was invited to perform with bands for weddings, dances, concerts, and more. This growing musical involvement enabled me to earn my way through high school, college, and dental school.

Music Lessons

I began taking music lessons from Mr. Herk Favilla utilizing a Stella guitar, which was close to the equivalent of "playing guitar on a telephone pole." It was difficult to manage. During this time, I also began studying the basics of classical theory. It just so happened that Mr. Favilla and his brother started making guitars and thought that I could benefit from playing on a more manageable instrument. They brought one of their "homemade" guitars to show me. It was a flat top, round hole, nice-sounding guitar at the cost of $75. My parents couldn't afford it. Mr. Favilla thought he might have a solution to this obstacle. The next week he returned with another Favilla guitar priced at $40. Minor point: there were two vertical cracks in the body of the instrument. Mr. Favilla assured us that the cracks would not get any bigger and the sound would not be affected. So, I got the guitar with the cracks. It is still in my possession, and it never got worse! Other major guitar manufacturers were becoming more popular with electronics and fancy designs, such as Gibson, Fender, and Gretsch. On the other hand, Martin guitars have maintained their traditional flat top style and fine sound since 1833.

John D'Angelico's Shop

After a period of time, I advanced, studying with Mr. Al Perlis and progressed through the Mel Bay's Modern Guitar Method, Grade 7 Level. I needed and wanted an upgrade for my next instrument. He firmly guided me to consider a D'Angelico guitar made in Little Italy at 39 Kenmare Street.

Many great guitarists, who happened to be in the New York

area, congregated at John D'Angelico's shop on Saturday afternoons. He would offer a shot of his favorite Scotch, J&B, to clients and hastily wipe clean the shot glasses with the dirty apron

he had been wearing all week. Of course, the Scotch would kill any bacteria remaining.

One Saturday we went to John D'Angelico's small dusty shop where several instruments were under various stages of construction. As the afternoon progressed, several older guitarists drifted in. I looked and listened in awe as I was introduced to Chet Atkins, Johnny Smith, and Les Paul. I couldn't believe it. Even though these brilliant masters may have advertised for other guitar manufacturers, they played and treasured D'Angelicos. I began to realize what a real quality guitar was. It wasn't just a beautiful piece of furniture with strings; it resonated, producing excellent tone, clarity, and sustain.

Al Perlis, my father, and I made a return visit to 39 Kenmare Street and discussed the possibility of a D'Angelico made to order for me. John suggested a slightly smaller-bodied, blond Excel cutaway model. The original invoice was $550, and it would take 12 to 18 months to complete. Payment would be made upon completion of the guitar.

During this interim period, I needed another decent instrument since I was playing gigs, such as weddings and dinner parties, enabling me to begin saving in anticipation of the completion of my custom Excel. John D'Angelico said he would find me a loaner guitar until mine was ready. He located a Gibson L-7

Jazz guitar great Chuck Wayne with his Benedetto custom instrument

guitar in a pawnshop in the East Village and suggested that I take a look at it. The pawnshop owner was asking $125 for it. I said I was a student and asked if he could include a case for it. He reluctantly agreed. I then said that I needed a D'Armond pickup and asked if he could throw in a strap for the $125 price. Well, all hell broke loose, and he chased me out of his shop, yelling that he wouldn't sell me the guitar no matter the price.

I returned to John's shop and told him what had happened, adding that *I needed the guitar*. He chuckled and said he would call the pawnshop owner and buy the guitar to be used as a loaner. I thanked John profusely, and in a few days, I had the L-7, with a case, pickup, and strap for my use.

I stopped by 39 Kenmare Street several times a month to see which guitarists were in town or to offer to run errands and sweep the floor. John and his assistant, Jimmy D'Acquisto, always had an abundance of repairs to make. I met Peter Yarrow, of the trio Peter, Paul and Mary, dropping off one of his folk guitars for a modification. He requested a block be cut out where the neck of the guitar joined the body of the guitar and a matching cover. This created a perfectly normal-looking secret compartment. I can only assume that some *medicinal quality* items might have been stored there.

On another one of my visits, I met Chuck Wayne. While getting into a cab, he had snapped the head off of his D'Angelico guitar, and it needed a repair. I studied with Chuck when I returned from Vietnam, from 1971 to 1973, and we remained close friends until his death in 1997. He visited me many times. Chuck greatly admired women, saying that the Spanish Moss hanging from the oak trees reminded him of southern women

**The author working with
Dion (circa 1961)**

**Reunion with the author
and Dion later in life**

**The author working with
Chubby Checker (circa 1962)**

**Jazz great
Bucky Pizzarelli**

swaying in the breeze.

I also met Bucky Pizzarelli in John's shop and became a long-time acquaintance of his. During my studio gigs, I played rhythm guitar with Bucky on several recordings. I became friends with many of the doo-wop singing groups in Brooklyn, and these friendships gave me the opportunity to record with them at Bell Sound Studios on 52nd Street in Manhattan. Under the direction of noted A&R (Artist and Repertoire) men Eddie Kissack and Teacho Wiltshire, I made several key musical acquaintances.

At the age of 16, I became a member of Local 802 of the American Federation of Musicians, which enabled me to get studio dates for background recordings as well as to accompany popular entertainers. Other aspects of my musical career included playing with Dion, Tony Orlando, and Little Anthony and the Imperials. Throughout life, music has enabled me to enhance my personal contacts. It truly is a universal language.

School Years

I completed primary education at Public School 186, middle school education at P.S. 227, and secondary education at New Utrecht High School—all in Brooklyn. It is worthy to note that up until this time, many schools were in a six-block radius: walking distance. There was a low crime rate probably because the school district defined the close-knit neighborhood.

Upon completing the seventh grade, I was designated as an SP or Special Progress student, meaning that I skipped the eighth grade and went on to complete high school. This was determined by academic performance.

I was also involved in extracurricular activities and was voted the best dressed, best musician, most likely to succeed, and most popular. Last but not least of all, I was president of the senior class. This is all true and not dreamed up by my proud mother. Ha ha!

After school was out for the summer, we spent our days lifting weights and playing sports at vacation day school centers. However, a major summer activity was escaping to Coney Island Beaches via the West End elevated train line to the last stop. Our group of friends congregated at Bay 15 on the beach and "under the boardwalk." There were always portable radios blaring out music from rhythm and blues, doo-wop, country, and Latin stations. Dancing on the beach included the lindy, cha-cha, mambo, the stroll, and the hop or you could relax on your beach blanket and soak up the rays. We formulated various types of tanning lotion ranging from baby oil and iodine to pure olive oil. For 50 cents, we could spend a great day that included subway fares, a soft drink, and a "knish" or pizza slice.

Brooklyn College, UMDNJ, and Carmel

In the twelfth grade, I applied to Brooklyn College and was accepted. I also was fortunate to receive a New York State Regents Scholarship, of which only 500 students were awarded in the entire state. Since Brooklyn College was tuition-free, I used my state scholarship stipend to purchase books and other items at my discretion. The financial benefit allowed my parents to prepare for my brother's college entrance two years behind me.

I entered Brooklyn College in 1961 and soon realized the high degree of competition needed to maintain enrollment. It was the finest of the New York City colleges. The minimum acceptance grade was a 90 percent high school average, and more than 20,000 students were in attendance.

Studying hard was a requirement, and a social life was virtually nonexistent. I had my own desk in the basement of the library, where I studied each night until closing time. I then took two connecting busses to get home. Occasionally, some classmates and I would "pull an all-nighter" in an empty classroom to prepare for an exam the following day. I stuck with it, and I guess it paid off.

I graduated from Brooklyn College in June 1965 with a double major degree in biology and chemistry. My application to dental school was dependent on tuition, room and board, location, and class size. All factors considered, I applied to New York University (NYU), Columbia, University of Medicine and Dentistry of New Jersey (UMDNJ), and Temple dental schools. I was accepted by all of them and discovered that medical and dental schools did not usually reject applicants from Brooklyn College.

The fact that there were rarely any rejections attested to the high esteem Brooklyn College held in the national scholastic ranking. By evaluating all parameters previously mentioned, I narrowed my final selection to NYU and UMDNJ. Because of smaller class sizes, tuition, and the fact that I could live at home, I chose to attend UMDNJ.

Perhaps the most significant aspect of my decision to attend had nothing to do with dentistry but with my desire to be closer to my high school and college sweetheart, Carmel Gallo.

The carpool for the dental class of 1969 began by meeting at my house; it was the most direct route from which to meet and depart. Four of us from Brooklyn gathered in our spotless white shoes, creased pants, and clinic jackets. My mother checked each of us, making sure we looked immaculate and passed inspection before we arrived at the dental school. For the most part, our carpool consisted of Ira Zohn, Frank Puccio, Marc Chalkin, and me.

Our classes at UMDNJ were a mix of basic sciences: anatomy, chemistry, pharmacology, and others, which combined medical and dental students. The pace of instruction was fast and comprehensive.

Dr. Frank Frates was the iconic symbol of the dental school. He was also known as "the Coach," the director of clinics at UMDNJ. As a retired naval captain, he insisted on excellence and shaped the lives of those he touched. Unlike other health professionals, the Coach made sure that we wore clean, crisp trousers and clinic jackets, and spotless white shoes. He enforced the principle: "If you can't get something right the first time, when will you have the time to do it again?" Our dental class started with 59 students but graduated 32 with DMD degrees. This attests to the fact that *the price of being the best, carries significant responsibility*. The Coach inspired many people. I am proud to have been a FTM (Frates Trained Man).

On a lighter note, Dr. "Fat Leo" Shatz, a clinical instructor, came into our practical anatomy lab the day after Thanksgiving eating a turkey drumstick, which he casually placed in his pocket. At the same time, he examined an anatomy specimen and then resumed his snack amidst the cadavers.

Carmel Gallo was the only girl in a family of seven older brothers. We lived about four blocks apart, attended the same high school, and graduated from Brooklyn College one year apart. Our circle of friends and family approved of our relationship. Carmel, being the only girl in her family, had to put up with lots of joking and teasing. Her parents were "old school," and I don't think we had an official date until she was 18 years old. Her father had passed away prior to that time.

Several years into our courtship, her uncle jokingly asked, "Sandy, so what are your intentions?" Mrs. Gallo stated, "Carmel is ready to get married." This was all done in a light-hearted manner, but I understood the subtleness. I was working as a musician and music teacher in addition to continuing my dental education. Carmel had graduated from Brooklyn College and had begun her career in teaching. We were married on August 21, 1966. With both of us working, we rented a small but comfortable studio apartment on Staten Island. Our life at the time was simple and enjoyable.

The last two years of dental school were clinically oriented, exposing me to many areas of patient care. A cousin, Catherine Termotto, had Down syndrome and special needs. She was receiving supervised neglect from dentists not trained in this discipline. I arranged for her to be seen in the pedodontic clinic for a thorough evaluation by two dentists who had training in sedative management. I was impressed with the results and decided to pursue this specialty in future postgraduate training after spending two years in the military. Providing comprehensive care to special needs patients has been a gratifying part of my professional career.

Making Money and Dealing with Debt

When I prepared to enter dental school, it became apparent that, despite being awarded various scholarships and financial aid packages, I needed additional monies to cover expenses. From an early age, I had always worked and taken many types of odd jobs to help make ends meet.

I would do minor jobs for "well-respected" men. One of those men, Joey Heart, asked me to fly to Cleveland and drive a brand-new Cadillac Eldorado Brougham back to Brooklyn. He then invited me over to his home and took me aside to thank me for doing this favor for him. He pulled out a bag filled with about 20 fine watches. Joey had a lot of connections in the jewelry exchange, and people owed him a great deal of money, so instead of cash they paid him with in-kind repayments. He told me to pick out whatever watch I wanted. There were many with diamonds and fine features, but I chose a less ornate but beautiful Jules Jurgensen watch with an 18-karat gold band and a thin face. Fifty-four years later, it still looks good and runs well. Joey then picked out a beautiful ladies' watch with diamonds and said: "Give this to your wife." I had been married for about two years. I guess this is why they called him Joey Heart.

During this time, my father had been unable to control his gambling habit, so I went to a lending agency and took out a loan for $5,000 to help pay off some of his debt. He still owed more than $20,000 plus the interest. I approached a friend, who was a "made man" with the Gambino family, and told him what was going on. He arranged a sit-down with the loan sharks who were associated with the Genovese family. Big John, a capo with the Genovese family, represented the loan sharks (also known as "shylocks") for the meeting. My friend proceeded to explain my father's habit and requested that the debt be forgiven or reduced. Big John said the best they could do was to stop the interest from accruing, but my father must still pay back the money owed. The word went out on the street that nobody was to loan my father a nickel because they would not get it back.

Someone then told me that they had read about guys making excessive amounts of money in the black market in Vietnam. I thought about going into the army and researching the possibilities of earning beyond my salary, helping to pay off my father's debt. Of course, I did not tell anyone about this.

The war in Vietnam was raging, and I was inducted into the Early Commissioning Program while I was still in dental school.

Basic Training

In June 1969, I received my DMD degree and after graduation, I left for Basic Training at Fort Sam Houston, San Antonio, Texas. I was told it would be beneficial if I arrived late for Basic Training because the BOQ (bachelor officer quarters) would be full. I arrived late and was put up at this great hotel with a swimming pool, tennis courts, and everything I could want. This hotel was also the home base for the American Airlines pilots and stewardesses. I was sitting at the bar by myself, and a stewardess sat next to me. She started a conversation by saying, "Captain, I just love uniforms." *Welcome to the Army and San Antonio.*

Intensive Basic Training took place in 110-degree heat. A team of two participants was given a goat to feed and look after for several weeks. At the end of this period, the goat was tied to a post, and we had to shoot it. The purpose of this was twofold: to see how we would react psychologically and to teach us how to debride a gunshot wound and stop bleeding under real-life battlefield conditions.

Another part of the training was live firing from foxholes. There was one guy who was always pushing to get into the first starting position. He was the first man into the foxhole, and we immediately heard screaming. The foxhole contained many scorpions. An ambulance came, and they carried him away. As he was leaving, the other trainees were cheering to teach him not to be so pushy.

During Basic Training, a group of officers would frequently dine at the *then*-newly opened Rhine Steakhouse on the River Walk in San Antonio. It is *now* designated the "Historic Rhine Steakhouse." Where did all those years go?

Advanced Oral Surgery Training

I arrived at Fort Jackson in Columbia, South Carolina in 1969 for advanced oral surgery training. Carmel and I settled into a pleasurable lifestyle with other young dental officers and their wives. Living in a disciplined, rank-oriented society was totally different for me. I was used to dealing with people regardless of rank. I was not concerned with "mickey mouse" regulations. If a man performed well, he gained my respect. I did not care if his hair was one-eighth inch too long. I did not pull rank, and I did not expect that of anyone else.

I enjoyed my colleagues even though their backgrounds were so much different than mine. On Friday and Saturday nights, I would go to the Officers' Club with my guitar and sit in with the band, allowing me to make new friends. During my off time, I enjoyed Lake Murray, and I decided to learn to fly. I was able to go to Shaw Air Force Base, near Sumter, and I joined the Aero Club. I worked hard and earned my pilot's license. I thought I could help support our troops and wanted to become involved in a war that would make history. *I believed in the U.S. and its commitment to fight communism.* I opposed the "hippies" and the anti-war sentiment.

Soon after settling in, members of my class began receiving orders to go to Vietnam; I confidentially approached my commanding officer, Colonel J. Ryan Jessel and told him that I wanted to volunteer for Vietnam. He called in the 1st Sergeant Robbie Robinson to witness my desire to volunteer. They said I would receive my orders with my class so as not to make my volunteering obvious, as I did not want my wife to know the situation. I thought I could help support our troops and wanted to become involved in a war that would make history.

I continued to learn as much as I could from the men returning from Nam about life over there. Finally, my orders to go to Vietnam arrived, and I realized that I would have to go through with this plan. It was somewhat disconcerting, especially since I had been watching combat footage on the TV evening news.

A Note Regarding General Hollingsworth

General James Hollingsworth was a club regular who enjoyed my guitar playing, and we became friendly. I learned that he had served in Vietnam. On occasion, we would close the club, change clothes, have breakfast, and go hunting. He was a gung-ho two-star general, but more importantly, he was a down-to-earth person. He and I spoke at length regarding the war.

Farewell Party

I had a 60-day leave prior to going to Vietnam so I went home to see my family. I made an arrangement that I would send back my earnings, in the form of money orders, which would be paid to the shylocks. My father was trying to help pay off his gambling debts by working two jobs.

Before leaving for Nam, my family had a farewell party to send me off, where everyone said goodbye and gave me gifts. A couple of my older uncles, who were WWII vets, jokingly told me about oriental women and their experiences. I held it together until I had to kiss my grandmother and grandfathers goodbye. I broke down, thinking that they may not be alive when, and if, I returned. *I never thought about my safety.*

Taking Off to Vietnam

My wife and brother drove me to JFK Airport, where I caught my flight to Travis AFB in California. My carry-on baggage included my personal S&W .38 Special since this was before terrorists and an officer was permitted to hand-carry a personal weapon to Vietnam, my Martin D-18 guitar, a Fender Bassman Amplifier, and a duffle bag containing six feet of chain and a lock. I took this thinking I could chain my guitar and stuff together when I napped so no one would steal them.

I also had five $100 bills so I could begin my "business" once I got situated in Vietnam. In California, I was transported by bus to a motel outside Travis AFB to spend the night. I got lucky. The motel had an Italian restaurant, and the owner was from

Sicily. As I sat at the bar eating my dinner, we began a conversation about my Sicilian background. Surprisingly the restaurateur knew of my grandfather's town in Sicily, and he graciously refused to accept payment for my charges.

The next day I reported to Travis AFB and got checked in. As we boarded Seaboard World Airlines, I heard voices calling me. I turned to look and saw two lieutenant dietitians from Fort Sam Houston. They had received a copy of my orders and flew to Travis AFB to say goodbye. I gave them a thumbs-up as I boarded the plane.

As we taxied down the runway, everything became very quiet. You could have heard a pin drop. Nobody spoke as we looked out the windows, and the plane lifted off. Reality struck home, and we wondered if we would ever return, or if we would die in a strange land. The stewardesses attempted to perk us up with games like "guess our bust sizes," etc. We were just a bunch of young warriors thrown together for transport, not in units as was done in WWII, and not knowing what destiny held for us.

We left the U.S. behind and had a stop in Taiwan. A friend, Captain Mark Zen Yamamoto, who went through Basic Training with me, was stationed in Taiwan. I called to tell him that I had a layover, and he met me at the airport so we could catch up. Mark chose to spend a posh tour of duty in Taiwan and met me in his new Datsun 240Z sports car. *I made my decision to volunteer to go to Vietnam and was headed to a combat zone. I had a family commitment to fulfill.*

3
VIETNAM STORIES

I arrived at the 90th Replacement Battalion in Tan Son Nhut, Vietnam, and it was very hot with 100-percent humidity. Sleeping was impossible. I used my chain to lock up my guitar, duffle bag, and amplifier so that no one could steal my stuff. The next morning, we were advised of the federal in-country laws. We had to turn in our "greenback" dollars for military pay script, also known as "Monopoly money." It was now illegal to possess greenbacks because of the high exchange rate on the black market. According to my research concerning the black market dealings, I faced a very sobering decision: turn in my five $100 bills or secretly keep them until I could establish my money-changing business.

The next day, all-new in-country personnel were processed for departure to their base camp assignments. I was the last remaining soldier to receive an assignment, and a 1st Sergeant approached me and said, "Sir, I'm looking for a Japanese captain named Terrimoto." I said, "Sergeant. That's me; I'm Italian. My name is Termotto."

We gathered my belongings and joined a convoy to Cu Chi. It was northwest of Saigon and close to the Cambodian border. We departed for Cu Chi on Highway 13, also known as Ambush Alley. This road was notorious for its many sharp curves, which kept it slow-moving and thus a bad place for possible ambushes. Due to its geographic shape, this area along the Cambodian border was referred to as the Fish Hook and Parrot's Beak.

As we moved toward our destination, an irritating, pungent odor permeated the air. The 1st Sergeant explained that the odor was from human feces being burned with diesel fuel since there was no plumbing. The lowest people on the military totem pole were the shit burners. *I can still smell it.* (Chicken wire was draped over everything where the American troops congregated to prevent the enemy from lobbing explosives at us and disappearing.)

After a hot, dusty, and tense ride, we arrived at Cu Chi. I met most of the guys and realized they were expecting a Japanese man named Terrimoto. The guys and I had a laugh and talked a bit since I had shown up with a guitar, amplifier, and duffle bag. It was unusual for a soldier to show up with this kind of baggage. My attention then shifted to an Italian captain named Joe Valenti. During our introduction, he asked me where I was from "back in the world" (a phrase commonly used in reference to home, or the U.S.). When I told him I was born in Tampa but raised in Brooklyn, he couldn't believe it. He said he was born and raised in Tampa. Our families knew some of the same people. I asked, "Do you know the name Santo Trafficante?" He mentioned his family acquaintance with the Trafficante family. My maternal grandfather had been a longtime friend with Santo Senior. I told him that I was baptized in Santo's home.

Next, I mentioned the family of Dr. Frank Adamo, a well-known WWII hero who survived the Bataan Death March. My mother and father lived in Dr. Adamo's carriage house after I was born. My father was in the Army stationed at MacDill Army Airfield in Tampa. Joe and I could have gone on, but I needed to unload my gear and find a hooch. I began by taking charge and asking, *or telling*, the group of guys where I wanted my stuff taken and told them, "Be careful." (To this day, Joe Valenti does a great imitation of the first time we met—including my bossy directions.)

A hooch is a crude shelter made with discarded Styrofoam rocket boxes, plywood, and some corrugated metal roofing that we scrounged up. We slept on six-inch thick mattresses laid on top of plywood. Fifty-five-gallon drums were filled with dirt and surrounded us for protection—a real architect's nightmare.

On any given occasion, the call "INCOMING" indicated enemy mortars or rockets were headed for us. We went to the relative safety of our bunkers as soon as possible. Our more seasoned GIs would joke about not having buttons on the front of their shirts due to the *30-mile an hour crawl* to safety. Cu Chi earned the moniker Rocket City due its high level of enemy activity and the frequency of attacks.

During one such attack, a GI named Riley was sitting on a barstool in a bunker. Afflicted with narcolepsy, he had fallen asleep during the attack and slipped off the stool, which resulted in a broken arm. He was eventually awarded a Purple Heart for his fall off of the barstool.

In February 1970, as the Vietnamese New Year (TET) celebration approached, things were pretty quiet. We had been on Red Alert anticipating that "sappers," or enemy soldiers carrying satchel charges, would attempt to penetrate our perimeter with explosives. Napalm was called in to burn all the vegetation surrounding us, which historically turned out better than defoliating with Agent Orange. A minefield was set up about 200 yards from our hooches in addition to concertina wire. The area outside of which was known as "Injun" or Indian country. However, we had four incoming rockets hit outside our perimeter.

In another incident, we had a close call from our own artillery due to a premature burst from a nearby fire support base. Shrapnel came through several hooches, but no one was injured. These are things that can happen in a combat zone.

During one such attack, my guitar was "wounded" by a stray piece of shrapnel. I thought about refinishing the entire guitar but decided to leave it, scratches and all, due to my lack of finances. At that time, it would have cost $85. The little imperfections bring back memories. I subsequently had the shrapnel hole repaired when I returned home from Nam.

40th KJ Medical/Dental Detachment

Cu Chi was a base camp with limited amenities. I was assigned to the 40th KJ team that consisted of some medical and dental personnel. Our motto, "preserve the biting strength," meant keeping troops in the field with relatively healthy oral tissues. In some instances, we were on call 24/7. In addition, our team worked to gain the hearts and minds of the South Vietnamese via civic action. Our KJ designation meant we had the mobility to go into villages to provide medical and dental treatment. The Department of the Army did not publish any information on our detachment due to the fact we had mobile status. This is where I met Dave Shealy, a SP-5 medic, who was assigned to the same unit. (Hopefully, this information can clarify work variations because our personnel were "attached" as needed for different missions.) Cambodian operations were always denied, but we occasionally knew that we were on Cambodian soil.

Once while driving slowly through Bien Hoa on a KJ mission, kids instantly surrounded our jeep. A "cowboy" (a thief on a motorcycle) skillfully snatched my watch from my wrist

Working hard to save the medically evacuated wounded

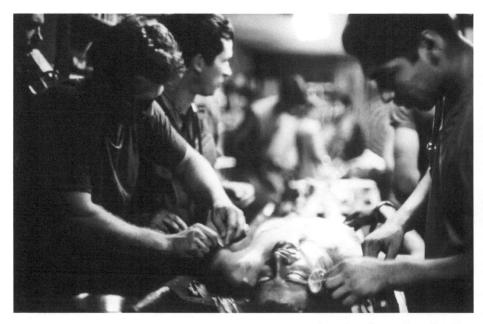

Combat Operating Facility

and made off with it. I instinctively drew my pistol and started to give chase, but my driver said, "Let's get the hell out of here since there are no other Americans around." It was a good move to "didi mau," the Vietnamese phrase meaning "go quick." The army considered that a combat loss and reimbursed me for $54. Not bad since I had only paid $38 for the watch.

The many Americans stationed in-country had widely versatile duties in the war-torn nation. Two of the most heated cries during their tour were: "INCOMING" and "VOLLEYBALL!" Incoming needs no clarification, but volleyball was the national sport of GIs, played even during monsoon months. Some troops never encountered "incoming!" or other combat-related experiences. It was estimated that only one in six personnel saw combat during their tour of duty; all other personnel were in support roles.

Upon returning from a mission, we needed recuperative time. Occasionally we watched movies. Our movie screen was a suspended white sheet. The troops manning the film reels often got distracted smoking pot. For example, reel number one was not always followed by reel number two, or reel number four might be in the number-two slot. In other words, the night's movie became very confusing, especially to the stoned GIs.

Every two or three weeks, the enlisted men and officers would gather in the compound for a cookout. Major Ed Santa, our XO (executive officer), was in charge of these events. I made sure we had food, usually chicken but sometimes steak. We had warm beer, Schlitz or Hamm's, but sometimes we had brown whiskey as a treat. As the evening wore on, we would sit around drinking beer, telling stories, and having a few laughs. I sat with

Dave Shealy and Tampa Joe, talking about the events of the week while Major Santa walked around asking us questions and engaging us in conversation. Three of the men sitting near us were red-faced, bent over like old men, and showing no signs of life. Major Santa asked us, "What's with those guys?" Dave replied, "Sir, they are drunk." Dave, Tampa Joe, and I started laughing because we knew they were stoned and drunk. They were escaping the reality of being in Vietnam. At the end of the night, Major Santa made Dave drag each of the three enlisted men back to the hooch area and deposit them. Another day in the "Jolly Green," also known as Vietnam.

Some of the better-connected officers had "girlfriends" they rendezvoused with for a "shot of leg." Once a month, usually around payday, we were visited by the Donut Dollies (Red Cross Nurses) for light social conversation and to listen to our band. The ranking officers spent the most time with them. Donut Dollies who were not very good looking were called Pastry Pigs. Some of the enlisted men saved up their money for the Red Cross "girls" who wanted to make some extra cash; thus they were named Bunker Bunnies. No explanation needed. This socializing ended when one Bunker Bunny was found dead, stabbed 10 times. An intensive investigation was done to no avail. After this incident, no women were permitted in the base camp.

Base Camp Tensions

Anything could happen in a combat zone with weapons, drugs, and racial tensions that complicated matters and occasionally led to "fraggings," or tossing fragmentation grenades at friendly troops to settle disagreements. One morning at about 2 a.m., a hooch was targeted by a fragmentation grenade. A lieutenant was killed and another badly wounded. I don't know exactly what happened, but I think some maniac had a run-in with the victims. Aside from watching out for "Charlie," someone on drugs could snap under stress. It was not a wise move for officers and troops to cause personnel problems. Everybody had to watch their backs. They caught the guy who fragged the lieutenants. The suspect was a "soul brother" with a police record a mile long and who had been a member of the Black Panthers before coming to Nam.

Our KJ team de-escalated an incident where two officers were putting each other up for medals that they did not deserve. This resulted in a lot of outraged men who risked their lives every day, while these two officers were afraid to leave the base camp. Since plumbing was very sparse, we urinated into 50-gallon drums that extended above ground level about eight inches. These were called "pissers." Some officers, who were not well-liked, had a habit of urinating prior to going to sleep. Someone conceived the idea to pour about a quart of gasoline into the pisser. As they proceeded to relieve themselves, some unknown person flipped a cigarette into the pisser. There occurred a mini-explosion that mostly burned their clothes and very nearly their private parts. The cigarette flipper was never found!

This was much less severe than the possibility of fragging. Another incident meant to inflict fear into a wrong-doer's mind happened after midnight when a disliked lieutenant was fast asleep. The door to his hooch was quietly barricaded, and the hooch set on fire. The deserving soldier was trapped inside with no way out. He was screaming. After a few minutes, "we saved his life" and dragged him out. He was very grateful to us for "rescuing him." No one could figure out how his hooch caught fire.

While in Vietnam, I adopted two kittens as pets to enjoy. One was black and named Super Pussy, and the other was a tabby I called Stud. We also had a community dog mascot we called Tiger. To feed the cats, my parents sent me cases of liver cat food while the dog ate leftovers.

Other lighter moments while living at Cu Chi included incidents directed at soldiers that were hard-core and strictly by the book. Our 40th KJ team had an excellent record of achievement and received various commendations that were scheduled to be presented at a formal ceremony. Our commanding officer knew I had many connections to obtain steaks, shrimp, chicken, and other edibles that would make him look good when he hosted a reception. He approached me and asked if I could handle the event. Of course, I agreed and began to contact my food resources and arranged for The Real Thing, our musical band, to perform. Since I needed some hors d'oeuvres for the event, I decided to use a case of cat food from my parents to make a great surprise delicacy—liver pate using blended chicken-liver cat food and crackers. I thoroughly enjoyed observing the delicious delicacy being eaten by all. The commanding officer received many compliments on the creative menu and terrific music.

Another light moment involved the dog, Tiger, and a stuffed-shirt captain who enjoyed relaxing and smoking his pipe every chance he got. After lunch, he would place his pipe down and go to the latrine. Tiger left some dried excrement in the area. Someone came up with the idea of mixing chopped dog droppings in with the captain's pipe tobacco. He loved smoking Tiger's dried and flavored poop.

Making the Best Out of Cu Chi

I had heard that places like Long Binh and BOQ 1 (officers' quarters) had swimming pools, restaurants, and even "round eye" nurses to share these luxuries with, all within about 15 miles from Cu Chi. We couldn't have it all, but I thought we could at least have a swimming pool: one out of three isn't bad for living at Cu Chi. We connected with some engineers and managed to get a 50-foot by 50-foot by 5-foot deep swimming pool dug and lined with one-half-inch thick black rubber. The interesting fact was that since the pool liner was black, you couldn't tell how deep the water was - it looked like a big black pit. We managed to get a rotor blade from a downed helicopter to use as a springboard. The engineers kept the water level up and voila! This was our answer to the beautiful, traditional pools at the bases in secure areas. *Where there is a will, there's a way, Cu Chi style.*

Unfortunately, it was not all fun and games. One of my kittens, Super Pussy, disappeared. I looked all over the surrounding areas and checked with everyone to no avail. I noticed a foul odor coming from behind my footlockers. I moved them away, and there was the kitten, hanging with its neck broken. Its belly was swollen, a horrible sight. It had been playing on top of my locker with one of her toys, a rabbit's foot, and had knocked it off behind the locker. In an attempt to get her toy, she had broken her neck. *This*

Group photo of the 40th Medical Detachment

Cu Chi with the Black Virgin Mountain in the distance

shook me up. The remaining kitten, Stud, was very lonesome, but I vowed not to get another one.

Making the best out of Cu Chi was not easy since it was close to the Cambodian border. We didn't have much to compare it with and thought it was routine to stay up at night watching and listening to the war being fought beyond our extended perimeter. This included parachute flares and Texas Farts, which were the sounds of miniguns mounted on Cobra gunships as they swooped down on a firing run. They placed a round in every square foot of ground the size of a football field on each pass. Every fifth round was a red "tracer" to follow the line of fire and make things more accurate.

I followed the same nightly routine for getting ready for sleep at my hooch at Bien Hoa and Cu Chi. Before crawling into my bed, I sprayed my "fortress" thoroughly with DDT, which we got by the case. I then closed my mosquito netting and fell asleep while being serenaded by the war beyond the perimeter. While dozing off, I could hear the light rustling sound of roaches scampering around.

Upon waking in the morning, there was ample evidence that the DDT was doing its job by the vast number of dead roaches all over. Thorough shaking off all boots and clothing was required in the morning. I often wondered what the effects of breathing DDT all night would have on me. So far, I have been lucky!

Food in Nam

Dr. Joe Valenti was a musician, and we became lifelong friends. Joe's culinary skills and the cans of black beans sent

Rapelling into a LZ
(landing zone)

by his folks led me to nickname him Tampa Joe Beans. We will always remember his delicious black beans and rice.

Joe was also skilled at preparing pasta dishes for large numbers of guys in the area. He scrounged up a two-gallon kettle and a piece of metal screen to serve as a colander to drain the pasta out of the large pot. Certain food items were relatively easy to get from the Class 1 Yard (food distribution) at Long Binh. Tampa Joe let me know what we needed, and I delivered: "some eggs" became 24 dozen eggs; "some steaks" became cases of steaks; shrimp was obtained in dehydrated gallon containers. We boiled water and dumped in the shrimp. Our steaks were grilled over 30-gallon drums, covered with a piece of screen on top. We could only estimate rare, medium, and well done. We didn't complain about eating steak.

Giving away our excess food to other nearby units generated goodwill and bartering arrangements. In return, Military Intelligence provided refrigeration. I had great connections getting the large quantities of food but no major way to store the excess supplies. Thus, we and MI had a joint mutual benefit and some great parties. One of which was when we were surprised with a visit from a scantily clad Mamie Van Doran and her band. I got lots of pictures of that. Another MI party involved a band and a stripper. Some of the GIs had their eyeglasses removed and placed lenses first into the stripper's G-string. The GI, keeping his hands behind his back, had to slip his glasses on his nose and ears without using his hands. Interesting game, to say the least.

One of our best bartering partners was the CIA since many of them had been in-country for more than 10 years. They always needed penicillin, of which we had plenty. In exchange, they gave us liquor, whatever personal weapons we wanted, and they even flew me into Saigon (Ton Sonhut) for gourmet dinners at classy restaurants. There were still five-star restaurants remaining from the French Occupation of Vietnam. One restaurant, La Plage, had a menu that included breaded quail eggs and pheasant under glass.

Black Market

When I arrived in-country, I was advised of the federal law that all greenback dollars must be surrendered in exchange for military pay script. Since one U.S. greenback could be traded for $4 on the market, five greenbacks would yield $20—$500, what I had, would be turned into $2,000 in military pay script. Greenbacks, in the wrong hands, could be used to purchase weapons on the international market. This military script could also be used to purchase salable items. Those items could be sold on the black market for 15 to 20 times what was paid for them. The basic concept is doubling or tripling your original amount of money tax-free.

Staff Sergeant Waldemar Keyes was on his third tour of duty in Nam when we met in Cu Chi. He re-upped to prevent his son from being sent to Vietnam. Wald was an astute businessman and a card shark. We were a good team. He was a black enlisted man, and I was a white officer, so we covered plenty of ground in our financial dealings. We bought many refrigerators and air conditioners when personnel were leaving Nam and resold them at 250 percent or more profit. We had a good network going for buying and selling even extending to Saigon, where prices were higher on the market. Other avenues of generating income

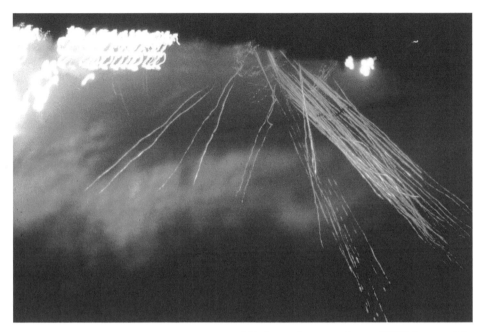

Mini gun tracers from COBRA gunship

were dealing in currency exchange and money lending at good rates. As soon as I got a large amount of money, I would loan it to other GIs in need. I did not charge any interest but requested it be paid back in the form of a money order to my brother or a friend back in the United States.

One morning at 6:30 a.m., it was announced that all financial transactions were frozen. This was known as C-Day or currency exchange day. All military pay certificates (MPCs) had been frozen, and new color currency, or "Monopoly money," was issued immediately. This was meant to trap people engaged in black market trading. Politicians and influential people who had excess old MPCs, would be hurt by the conversion since they could not hide their illegal monies. All old series MPCs were now worthless, and all currency transactions were watched closely. Fortunately, I was well-positioned and did not lose my money.

If a soldier was found to have more than $300 per month above his salary, he could be investigated for possibly dealing in the illegal black market. We had to launder the excess profits we made and get them out of the country. I had many family members and friends who would receive money orders sent in their names and cash them into a special account. They then sent me a photocopy of the transactions and more $100 bills enclosed in their letters. The cycle would start all over again. They received 10 percent back for their efforts.

Going back to my initial mission statement: I volunteered to go to Vietnam to pay off my father's debt and provide my family financial stability. I was successful, to say the least!

FAC/OV-10

While at Cu Chi, I became friendly with pilots in the 12th Aviation group. These pilots were FACS (Forward Air Controllers) flying O-1s or Bird Dogs, O-6 Skymasters, and OV-10 Broncos. I showed them my commercial pilot license that I had earned at Shaw AFB. Regulations were fairly relaxed, and as a captain who was a civilian aviator and who enjoyed flying, they were happy to have me fly second seat if our schedules coincided. I gave them preferred treatment when they needed dental work.

My favorite aircraft, the OV-10 Bronco, was a twin-engine "push-pull" high winged aircraft with front- and rear-ejection seats and no air-conditioning. Its ordinance consisted of 28 white phosphorus rockets that could pierce any known armor and four 7.62 mm M-60 machine guns. It was powered by two

The author flew FAC missions as a co-pilot in the OV-10 Bronco

715-hp turboprop engines, using opposite rotation for balance, and the top speed was 280 mph. The OV-10 used Wilson Picketts (also known as willy peeps), which were white phosphorus rockets to mark targets for our F4s, F5s, and Australian Canberra bombers 10,000 feet above us. After the targets were marked with white phosphorus, the areas were bombed, and the OV-10s went in low and slow to reconnoiter the damage. We often caught some ground fire. The pilot would perform a quick, evasive maneuver, frequently pulling 4 Gs to climb to safety.

My most memorable FAC mission began as a routine cruise

to check our fly area. The OV-10 we were flying had five radios monitored as follows:

Air to air

Air to ground

Air to home base

Air to artillery

Air to special operations groups or SOGs

We were cruising the area northwest of Tay Ninh in the Iron Triangle when we picked up the intense whisper of the call sign "Sly Fox."

"FAC one, this is Sly Fox. Can you read me?"

I responded, "Rodger that Sly Fox. You are in a triple canopy with no visible landmarks. Charlie is very heavy."

Sly Fox replied, "Don't hang around. Charlie will get suspicious."

We replied, "Have your best monkey climb a tree so he can possibly flash us with a ground mirror."

"FAC one, fly wide patterns and try to spot our flashing."

"We've got your flash," we replied. "Sit tight, and we'll plot your coordinates."

"FAC one to ground, there is a small clearing about 100 yards heading 90 degrees ESE."

"FAC one to ground, we're coming at you with 4 Cobra gunships armed with mini-guns and 2 Hueys for exfiltration of SOGs. The Cobras will cut the grass for you. Stay tight behind the mini-guns."

The SOGs (special operation groups) were instructed to tightly follow the path created by the mini-guns (6000 rounds/minute) for 100 yards to the clearing. Under cover from the

Cobra gunships, the Hueys then swooped down to pick up the SOGs. Once the troops were extracted, the bombers came in to obliterate the area. The OV-10s went in to assess the damage. They did a pretty good job, but many pissed-off "gooks" were left alive. We released our remaining white phosphorus rockets to mark targets and called in additional airstrikes. I guess the maneuvers to avoid the shit that "Charlie" was throwing at us made me a little nervous and nauseous.

The Calvary came to the rescue. The mission lasted about two hours, and we then returned to landing strips in Bien Hoa to count the bullet holes in the OV-10. I flew second seat on 13 missions over Vietnam, Laos, and Cambodia.

While stationed at Cu Chi, I was attached to the 1st Air Cavalry, which was in charge of expanding our areas of operation to secure them from the North Vietnamese Army (NVA) and Viet Cong, which included Bien Hoa. On one occasion, I flew down in a Military Intelligence chopper to Can Tho in the Mekong Delta on a special propaganda mission produced by the South Vietnamese Ministry of Health. It was a very insecure area and was overrun the night before. I hoped that it would be my last chopper ride to a hot area.

Cambodian Invasion

At the beginning of March 1970, Cu Chi became a strategic site as a springboard for the 1st Air Cavalry leading the Cambodian Invasion. This increased the level of combat in an effort to block the Ho Chi Minh Trail (The Communist Supply Line).

Areas such as Tay Ninh, Dau Tieng, Trang Bang, and others were now covered by both the 25th Infantry and the 1st Air Cavalry. The backside of Cu Chi approximated the Michelin

Rubber Plantation, and Nui Ba Den, better known as Black Virgin Mountain. The top of this mountain became a vital communication center of this area since the surrounding terrain was flat. Early on, one factor was overlooked: the sides of Black Virgin Mountain were honeycombed with NVA and VC tunnels. The only way to and from the mountaintop was by helicopter, weather and hostile fire permitting.

The Cambodian Incursion led to a finding that gradually explained VC disappearing into thin air around Cu Chi. An elaborate network of underground tunnels and chambers, including medical and living facilities, had been built underneath the base camp, dating back to the days of the French Occupation. "Tunnel Rats," small soldiers armed with pistols and flashlights, were sent into this network to flush out the enemy. Today, the Tunnels of Cu Chi are a major tourist attraction.

Bien Hoa

The 25th Infantry was gradually standing down at Cu Chi and moving to Bien Hoa with the 1st Air Cavalry. My closeness with the troops left me with no desire to leave Vietnam while they were still engaged in combat, so I eventually moved to Bien Hoa with the 1st Cavalry.

Serving together in a war zone to complete a specific task was of utmost importance regardless of rank. Ability, integrity, respect, and commitment were the qualities necessary to have a good team. Two of my most dependable enlisted men were Dave Shealy and Waldemar Keyes. Brother Dave was from Columbia, South Carolina, and had several military occupational services (MOSs) due to his cross-training. He was willing and available day or night to help in facilitating treatment for Vietnamese civilians. His civic action missions were successful. I resumed my duties, one of which was a civic action operation.

This was an account as experienced by SP-5 Dave Shealy, bravo-medic with the 40th Medical Detachment:

"Our destination was the village of Trang Bang. As we were leaving the 25th Infantry base camp at Cu Chi, the sun was just barely rising. The sergeant in charge of today's mission was driving a 3/4-ton truck. I was riding shotgun with my M-16 and M-79, 'thumper' or grenade launcher. We were part of a convoy heading towards a VC infested area. The lead vehicle was a truck loaded with Wolfhounds, 'infantry.' Their job was to set up a protective perimeter in the village in which we would be working.

When we arrived at the village, all the personnel and supplies were unloaded from the vehicle. On this trip, we had dental assistants, one Vietnamese dentist, one American dentist, and one

One of our bunkers that was overrun

combat medic. The Wolfhounds had already set up the perimeter around the village.

The sergeant in charge quickly realized that we had an excessive amount of personnel for the operation. He quickly ordered me to the field with the Wolfhounds. I grabbed my gear and headed out into the boonies around the village. As I headed down a small path, I noticed some villagers walking towards us for treatment. I spotted an older Mama-san on the path and stopped her to look at her injured arm. Her right arm was the size of my thigh. We asked her what had happened. She stated that during the TET offensive about one year ago, she was running for cover during a VC village raid, she fell and landed on her arm. I decided to call in a medevac chopper to our location to extract this woman to a surgical hospital in Saigon. She needed orthopedic surgery. The chopper arrived, and 20 minutes later, evacuated her."

After we arrived back at base camp, we went to my hooch to review the day. I had an A/C unit and a fridge with beer. After we covered the events of the day, Dave looked over at me, smiled, and said, "Another day in the Jolly Green."

Heart Attack

One afternoon in October 1970 at Cu Chi, Major Santa arrived in a chopper to tell me about my father's "death." He had my emergency orders. I got a couple of essentials in my duffle bag and was ready to leave. When Major Santa and Lieutenant Colonel Stahle put me on the chopper at Cu Chi, I was informed that I did not have to return to Nam due to my father's "death." I could not just leave my guys and take the easy way out. I told them to secure my stuff and that I would return to Nam.

I found out at a layover in Japan when I called my wife, Carmel, that the Red Cross was misinformed. My father was *near death and not dead*. My emergency orders gave me clearance to travel in my jungle fatigues, and within 28 hours I went from Cu Chi to Fort Dix, New Jersey.

I deplaned at Fort Dix; my brother was picking me up. I walked right by him—he did not recognize me. I had lost 25 pounds, and in my jungle fatigues and "booney" hat, I was a stranger. We finally connected, and he drove me directly to Maimonides Hospital in Brooklyn. People looked at me like I was from another planet. I didn't realize how strange it was to be back in the world. The people I encountered in New York City stared at me in my combat clothes. The culture shock I experienced was very significant considering I was coming from Nam and all that I had been through.

My father was in the cardiac intensive care unit hooked up to IV lines. He had been under tremendous stress, which undoubtedly contributed to his health problems. When my father saw me, he broke down and cried. I had very little emotional reaction and repressed my feelings. I was mentally exhausted, but I gradually got reoriented to my wife and family.

I reviewed my orders and noted that my leave was indefinite and that I did not necessarily have to return to Nam. My father's health improved, and within several weeks he was at home. I asked a friend to help me renegotiate my father's loans. I had been faithfully making payments from Vietnam, and I was favorably looked upon for keeping my word. As the days passed, my thoughts were constantly returning to my buddies that I had left behind, and I decided that I wouldn't let them down. I went to Fort Hamilton in Brooklyn and updated my emergency leave, enabling me to complete my tour of duty. *I was ready to get back to my unit. I didn't forget.*

In the meantime, there was a major power struggle between the Genovese family and the Gambino family regarding, among other things, the accountability for loan-sharking monies. A media news bulletin was issued stating that Big John, the Genovese loan shark I had been dealing with, was brutally murdered in a car bomb explosion. Most of his business records were destroyed, and our remaining loan was wiped out.

Memorable Christmas

I returned to Vietnam near the end of November. As Christmas 1970 approached, the troops increasingly thought of their loved ones at home and their buddies who had been killed or wounded in action. To dispel the holiday blues, we had planned to have a steak cookout on Christmas afternoon, but I figured that these brave young warriors deserved something better than a cookout to lift their spirits.

I thought about all the contacts I had made playing music with our band, The Real Thing, and I formulated a plan that would require some "deals" and a few $20 bills to the *right* people. I sought the needed contacts and arranged for them to look the other way when necessary.

Christmas morning, at sunrise, I was at the MP gate in a jeep, followed by my trusted Staff Sergeant Waldemar Keyes in a deuce and a half (a two and a half-ton) truck. The duty roster was revised to ensure the right MPs would be at the gate when we returned.

Early-morning traffic was light into Saigon. Our first stop was at an American Express office, where we sat and waited for 20 minutes. I began to sweat a little. Would our plans have to be aborted? Finally, a taxi pulled up, and three very attractive Vietnamese girls carrying small suitcases got out. We greeted each other enthusiastically. The girls were the employees of American Express and the first of several guests I had invited to brighten Christmas Day for my unit. After a few more stops at predetermined locations, I assembled 10 of the prettiest Vietnamese women I met during my tour. I assured them that they would be treated well and that they would have a great time. Pick-ups at rendezvous points were necessary since many Vietnamese would not permit their daughters to fraternize with American GIs.

Step two of my plan was to avoid harassment and arrest by the "white mice," so-called because all government law enforcement agents wore short-sleeve white shirts. It was illegal to have South Vietnamese nationals riding in U.S. Army vehicles. When we approached possible trouble spots, Staff Sergeant Keyes pulled alongside my jeep to screen us from the police's view as we quickly moved out of Saigon. We picked up speed and used our screening tactic successfully. Luckily, the MPs were quite busy directing traffic to the Bob Hope show that was going on at Long Binh.

As we approached the checkpoint to our base camp, I was greatly relieved to be hastily waved through by the MPs that I had arranged to be there. Normally, no Vietnamese citizens, other than workers, were permitted into our compound.

When we arrived at our hooches, I could see the troops moping around. We commenced blowing the jeep and truck horns, since we were without sleigh bells, and came to a skidding stop. The troops were startled, and I announced, loudly, that we were about to have a Merry Christmas. Our visiting guests donned their more comfortable "western attire," and the troops went to clean up. Before long, everyone was having a good time. I vividly recall the bright smiles, the laughter, and dancing that went on until dark. As far as I can remember, a good time was had by all.

I am glad that I broke tradition that day in a far-off land as many of these boys had no time to enjoy life. Some of them never saw another Christmas.

25th Infantry Division

1st Air Cavalry Division

4
MUSIC IN NAM

Much of my life experience in Vietnam intertwined with music and its effect on the mind. Whether it was about home "back in the world" or remembering fallen comrades, songs such as "Don't It Make You Wanna Go Home," the "Tennessee Waltz," or "Your Cheatin' Heart" summoned up memories. The following are several related quotes:

"You are the music while the music lasts." — T.S. Eliot

"Music is the art which is most nigh to tears and memories." —Oscar Wilde

"Country music is three chords and the truth." —Harlan Howard

"Music is what feelings sound like." —Author Unknown

"Music is an outburst of the soul." —Frederick Delius

Music opened up many doors for me and broadened my life experience a hundred-fold. My musical ability put me through college and dental school, and helped me to establish a dental practice. I accomplished all this while working as a studio musician, playing gigs and teaching music.

Over the years, I met a wide variety of interesting people who influenced me to decide whether or not to pursue a full-time musical career. I realized that many world-class musicians were struggling financially and leading less than desirable lifestyles. After weighing all factors, I chose dentistry. However, music remained a strong thread throughout my Vietnam experience, especially in regard to my friendship with Joe Valenti, who I initially met in 1969 upon arriving in Cu Chi.

I firmly believe we were destined to meet in Vietnam. The fact that I was born in Tampa immediately gave us common ground upon which to build our friendship. Joe's musical ability, combined with my love for music, enabled us to bring enjoyment not only to ourselves but also to the many people who experienced our performances. Joe and I began to play together, me on guitar and Joe on electric bass. Gradually we became known for our music.

Aside from handling oral surgery and dental cases at a small clinic, we often found ourselves with a lot of downtime. We converted downtime into rehearsal time, and Joe's vocals blended well with our guitar and bass. The guitar I carried to Vietnam was a Martin D18 with a DeArmond pickup. My amplifier was a Fender Bassman, which carried the sound well. Overall, we had a great balance. I had an extensive repertoire of music, and our sound was pretty much together. Word of our music spread, and we received a call from two colonels, both of whom were with the 12th Evacuation Hospital at the opposite end of Cu Chi. These officers heard about our music and wanted to meet us. We had one issue—a lack of transportation. They said not to worry, and we set up a time to meet.

A hospital Jeep arrived with plenty of bucking and stalling. Joe and I thought the two Colonels were going to destroy the vehicle since, as field grade officers, they had never driven a clutch drive Jeep before. Colonels Quinones and Diaz-Ball introduced themselves, and we had a good laugh! They mentioned that the 12th Evac hosted parties and invited us to provide the music. We agreed but checked with our commanding officer, Lieutenant Colonel Bill Stahle. He had a minor problem; he was a bit jealous since two colonels drove to meet two captains for a social invitation. Lieutenant Colonel "Wild Bill Stahle" had no objection after he, too, was invited.

The parties were a great success, and we made many connections as a result. At one party, a surprise occurred as I poured myself an amaretto. To my dismay, a two-inch-long roach that had been trapped in the bottle came out. Now, I always check my drinks.

It was not uncommon to see even colonels be moved to tears by songs of their home. Colonels Quinones and Diaz-Ball were from Puerto Rico and missed their families a lot. They asked if I could play some Latin tunes for them. I began by playing, "En mi Viejo San Juan." I never expected to see the two colonels break down and cry because they missed home. Colonels Quinones and Diaz-Ball were two of the most unforgettable people I met in Nam.

The Real Thing

On occasion, Philippino and Vietnamese bands would come through Cu Chi to perform at the "Snake Pit," which was a makeshift club lined with sandbags. Invariably their sound was very loud and distorted with excessive reverberation. Their inability to pronounce certain words, such as "reeba" instead of river, demonstrated their limited knowledge of the English language. I decided we should start our own group. We produced a good sound with me on lead guitar; Tampa Joe on electric bass and vocals; Jim Borovay, aka Rapper John, on rhythm guitar; Nelson Cass on drums; "Little Ernie"

Music By...

The Real Thing

Down To The Onion...

The Real Thing rehearsing with mattresses to baffle the sound

McClelland on tambourine, vocals, preaching, and dancing. Ernie was a great communicator with the audience, especially with the "soul brothers."

Since our sound was pure American, I had named the group The Real Thing, since we were not just a distorted imitation. Our business card said, "Down to the Onion" which was a phrase used in Nam to describe something enjoyable. We drank gimlets with onions. They claim that the best part of the drink was when you got down to the onion.

Music can be helpful in restoring the traumatized brain to a kind of order. It can transform perception, organize life experiences, and create a calming effect. We did not know it then, but this is what we were accomplishing with The Real Thing. It was an unrealized benefit at the time.

Our sound tightened up, anchored by Joe's solid bass and vocals along with my lead guitar. We set up a "recording studio" in an empty hooch, using mattresses suspended from the ceiling to act as a baffle, improving sound quality. The only drawback to our recording was interference every time a chopper flew over. We had to stop and start again. The tapes we made still sound pretty good, even four decades later.

On one of my R&R trips I traveled to Hong Kong, a beautiful city built on several mountainous islands. The airstrip is very narrow and juts out into the bay, leaving it surrounded on three sides by water. While there, I purchased Tom Jones-type outfits for the band. Economically, the dollar was strong.

In addition to band outfits, my family and friends had given me a list of requests for purchases to make when I took R&R. The bargains were great. I spent a fortune shopping and "sav-

The Real Thing performing at the 12th Evacuation Hospital

ing" money. My purchases included 23 watches, a TEAC 4010 tape recorder, a pair of Bose 901 speakers, and the list goes on. I still use the sound equipment after all these years. The best part was that I stayed at the Peninsula Hotel and was chauffeured around in a Rolls Royce. Not bad for a captain winding down his tour in Vietnam. While there, most importantly, I purchased a Fender Twin Reverb amplifier.

I flew Vietnam Airlines, which had a convenient and economic ticket, to return to Bien Hoa along with civilian mama-sons and papa-sons crowded into a non-air-conditioned twin prop engine plane.

My flight landed, and I deplaned only to be met by two white mice customs agents. Like most South Vietnamese officials, they were very corrupt. They asked to see my receipts and added a 100-percent import tax. I disputed this tax, and they confiscated my amplifier, holding it until I paid the tax. I told them that I was in Nam fighting for their democracy, and I wasn't going to be extorted. They had pistols, and I was unarmed, so I left. I was really pissed off. That night, I devised a plan to recover my Twin Reverb amp. I did not tell my commanding officer, Lieutenant Colonel Stahle, all the details, but I knew he enjoyed listening to The Real Thing and coming to parties. Knowing that his social life would benefit, he approved my glossed-over recovery plan. He told me, "Don't get hurt and don't kill anybody."

The next day—I, along with five enlisted men armed with M-16s— secured a deuce and a half. We headed directly toward the Vietnamese customs warehouse, where I knew my amp was stored. The day before, my surveillance indicated that none of the white mice had M-16s, just pistols. We pulled through the gate, and four of our armed enlisted men secured the area. We loaded the amp into the truck bed and drove off. The white mice realized they were outgunned and did not interfere. Lieutenant Colonel Stahle was very pleased that the amplifier was recovered with no casualties and no taxes paid.

Equipped and outfitted, The Real Thing played at memorable performances from 1970 to 1971 for dignitaries at various venues. One such performance celebrated the transition of General Michael Davison to the role of Allied Commander of European troops. His wife, Jean, was being flown in from the Philippines for her husband's ceremony. General Davison had requested that we play the popular song "Jean" as his wife stepped off her transport helicopter. The first chopper arrived and we started to play the request, but she was not aboard that one or the next. Finally, the third transport helicopter landed, and our group played "Jean," and General Davison welcomed his wife.

Other functions included celebrations for:

Ambassador Ellsworth Bunker
Ambassador Funkhouser
CIA Compound
USAID Compound
Military Intelligence Compound
Australian Compound
Long Binh Club
12th Evacuation Hospital
3rd Field Hospital
36th Medical Detachment

After one late party in Bien Hoa, our CIA hosts offered us a Bronco to drive back to our base. They would pick it up at a future date. This seemed to be the most efficient thing to do to get us back. After five minutes of driving, an MP vehicle flagged us down and ordered us to put our hands over our heads. We stopped, and I asked the two MPs what the problem was. They immediately called for reinforcements. They told us that we were in civilian clothes (white pants and Tom Jones shirts), it was after curfew in a combat zone, and our Bronco was a stolen vehicle. By this time, additional MPs arrived. They radioed to their commanding officer and told him that he would not believe this story. He had arrested four captains in civilian clothes, driving a stolen Bronco. We were then taken into custody for questioning at the MP station. The interrogation room was lit by a single, suspended light bulb that pulsed in sequence with the small generator powering it. This was enough to mesmerize you. They verified our story and confirmed it with the CIA. By this time, it was daylight, and we were taken to Long Binh to go before the chief Provost Marshall.

There we were in our white pants and blue shirts next door to the notorious Long Binh Jail. The Provost Marshall contacted our commanding officer at Bien Hoa and explained what had occurred. Lieutenant Colonel Stahle was furious, probably because he was not invited to the wild CIA party. I expressed my apologies for having caused this disturbance, albeit innocent. In my conversation with the Provost Marshall, I offered the services of The Real Thing. If he ever needed a band with go-go dancers, I would be happy to provide it at no cost. He accepted and said that since we were providing entertainment for the troops, he would grant us special IDs so that we could wear civilian clothes in conjunction with the musical performances. After things were ironed out, we offered to invite Lieutenant Colonel Stahle along in the future. Case closed with a happy ending. The Real Thing wins again.

We also played many concerts at various fire support bases. During one of our hasty landings at Phouc Vinh, an electric keyboard fell out of our chopper during a tight spiral landing. That was luckily our only combat loss.

5
SETTLING IN SAVANNAH

Toward the end of 1971, my commanding officer determined that I had had enough of Nam and gave me an "early drop." Essentially this meant: get your paperwork in order and be prepared to return to the world.

As I approached my departure (DEROS) date, items that were to be shipped home were reviewed. My .38 Special revolver that I legally carried into Vietnam could not be returned home because it was not considered a "sporting weapon." I certainly was not going to leave my sidearm behind. I carefully removed the rear panel of my TEAC deck and placed the gun inside. I replaced the rear panel and then shipped my tape deck back to the world. I still have that personal weapon to this day. Where there is a will, there is a way.

A Note Regarding Vic Aliffi

Other veterans and I did what we thought was right by supporting freedom and democracy. We were young and fought hard, never considering how the war would affect the rest of our lives. Many of us came away with significant amounts of baggage. We lead "normal" lives and are good citizens—but something still might remain in the back of our minds that can trigger a flashback.

One of the most memorable people I met while serving with the 1st Cavalry in Vietnam was Jay Victor Aliffi, known as Vic. It was a very hot day in Bien Hoa when Vic's unit came through our perimeter after spending a couple days in "Injun Country," what the Cav called everything outside our perimeter. He looked like a bandit with crisscross bandoliers of ammunition draped over his big frame and he carried a sawed-off shotgun.

The author's friend and most memorable war fighter, Vic Aliffi

Vic earned a reputation as a tough, no-nonsense soldier. He was awarded a battlefield commission to captain, two Silver Stars, eight Bronze Stars, a combat Infantry man's badge, and multiple other decorations. His military citations repeat the lines: "with complete disregard for his own safety." He was responsible for saving several lives and silencing the enemy.

After our initial meeting in Bien Hoa, Vic and I became fast friends, and I learned about his family in Savannah, Georgia. I invited him to some of our social activities. I chose them carefully since Vic was a remarkable soldier with an impeccable career that I wanted to protect from some of my escapades. He left the army in 1976 on a medical discharge. Vic Aliffi died of a brain tumor on May 18, 2002.

While Vic Aliffi remained in-country to complete his tour of duty, Carmel and I visited the Aliffi family. Vic's father, Jim, welcomed us and introduced us to the mayor, the sheriff, several bankers, and other prominent members of the community. I was most impressed by the reception we received.

Only then did I find out that Vic had earned a football scholarship to Clemson University. In 1969, his efforts garnered the notice of the NFL. He was a sixth-round draft pick for the Philadelphia Eagles with whom he played as a tackle.

During this trip, Carmel and I also visited Hilton Head Island and decided to invest some of our savings in a new development called Palmetto Dunes. Planning for the future, we purchased a third-row oceanfront lot for $15,000. People in New York thought we were insane and told us, "All they have are alligators and snakes on Hilton Head Island!" We were confident that the property would increase in value. I wish all my financial investments had been that good.

On returning to New York, we continued to work, and I pursued my postgraduate education. I began to reassess possible plans and passed the Georgia and South Carolina State Board Exams in Dentistry. We decided that professionally there was much more opportunity and a better lifestyle to be had if we moved.

Carmel and I strategically planned to embark on a new adventure. However, I did not anticipate the tremendous hardship facing Carmel since she was an only daughter leaving her mother and family. We would be the first of all the immediate families to leave the northeast.

Welcome Home from Nam

Upon my return from Vietnam in 1971, we lived in a studio apartment in Staten Island. I have never forgotten one incident as I was planning to go by bus to Fort Hamilton in Brooklyn. It was a rainy day, I was in uniform, and I planned to board the bus with a $5 bill. I was immediately informed that I needed exact change for my fare. The bus driver refused to let me on since I only had the $5 bill, and he would not provide change. I explained that I recently returned from Vietnam and was unfamiliar with new fare regulations.

People were getting impatient with the delay, so I asked the lady behind me if she would pay my exact change fare, and then she could keep my $5 bill as compensation for helping a Nam Vet. She paid my 50-cent fare and kept my $5 bill: Welcome home, Nam Vet.

Transitioning to Professional Life

Thanks to the efforts of Dr. Thomas Sinatra, Dr. Thomas La-Rocca, and Dr. Herbert Bartlestone, I gradually found employment when I returned to civilian life.

Dr. Sinatra assisted me in obtaining an appointment to practice as an acting oral surgeon on the staff of the International Longshoremen's Dental Clinic. This suited my extensive surgery training prior to and during my Vietnam tour. Dr. LaRocca gave me a position in his Brooklyn office, enabling me to practice various disciplines of general dentistry.

I set about learning the practice of fine restorative dentistry. The owner of Magna Dental Institute, the best lab in New York City, arranged for me to meet Dr. Bartlestone, associate dean of Columbia University Dental School. I explained my position, but Dr. Bartlestone said I would have to pay him $500 per day to observe in his office at One Eleven East 79th Street in Manhattan, a very upscale neighborhood.

I couldn't afford that amount, but he invited me to attend his annual, very limited invitation-only seminar at Columbia University. One day, Dr. Max Widrow, a former partner of Dr. Bartlestone, called me to his office and explained that a "mitzvah" had occurred: Dr. Bartlestone sustained an injury riding his bike and needed someone to assist with minor treatments. I agreed to help. Under Dr. Bartlestone's guidance, I learned a great deal and completed selected cases.

While increasing my professional involvement, I developed an interest in treating patients with special needs; my cousin, Catherine Termotto, who had Down syndrome, led me to apply for an advanced postgraduate course in sedative management. I was one of only two doctors to complete the program.

Upon completion of this course at New York University/ Brookdale Hospital, I had the credentials qualifying me to treat special needs patients requiring sedative management. I found providing dental care to special needs patients requiring sedation to be extremely gratifying.

The Move to Savannah from Staten Island

Carmel and I arrived in Savannah, Georgia on Labor Day 1974. With my mother-in-law's financial help, we purchased a home, complete with a pool, on Wilmington Island. Carmel taught school, and I practiced at the Beaufort-Jasper Comprehensive Health Center on a part-time basis.

I also treated patients a few days a week in Savannah and Hinesville, Georgia, building a broad patient base for the future. My objective was to make Savannah and Hilton Head my primary offices while gradually phasing out the others. The Hinesville patients continued to make the 35-minute drive to Savannah and comprised a solid core of the practice.

I was ambitious and confident, which did not sit well with the local dental community. I did my homework, "circled my wagons," and began practicing despite the conservative climate and hierarchy. Attitudes settled down as I exhibited my professionalism and genuine interest in providing quality dentistry. Within two years, I decided to open a satellite office on Hilton Head to accommodate my growing number of Carolina patients who traveled more than an hour each way to the Savannah office. This began a long-term relationship with the fine people I treated on Hilton Head. As the third dentist on the island, I built a productive base.

The History of Polo in the Lowcountry

In 1974, the upscale Hilton Head community welcomed polo as a unique addition to its golf and tennis lifestyle. The Hilton Head Polo Club began at Honey Horn Plantation. I was asked to become a founding member and accepted, thinking I might enjoy being around horses again. The other founding members included Frederick Hack, Bill Ruth, and Bill Roe. The advisory board members were General "Pony" Scherrer, General Sim Whipple, and Colonel Harry Wilson. Honey Horn was the center of polo through 1977.

There was a hiatus of polo in the Lowcountry until 1978 when a man from Virginia, Joe Claffey, built a polo field and an arena in Hilton Head Plantation. On Friday evenings, arena polo was played in a 100- by 50-yard area with four-foot-high sideboards. Sunday afternoons were reserved for regulation polo on the 300- by 160-yard field.

In 1980, I met Iva Welton, whose husband was a part-owner of Rose Hill Plantation, a developing equestrian community. Upon touring the property, I saw what potentially could be a fine polo field. It was groomed, reseeded, and given time to mature. The result was a first-class regulation field.

Iva Welton and I set out to resurrect polo in the Lowcountry. Players from Atlanta, Aiken, Charleston, and Palm Beach eagerly supported the fledgling Rose Hill Polo Club. Matches were held in the spring and fall. In the meantime, the Okatie Rotary Club was established and needed a source of revenue to support local charities. I proposed that the Okatie Rotary Club be the primary beneficiary of the polo matches at Rose Hill. This was financially successful, and Polo for Charity became

The author taking a jump, fox hunting with Dynamite

The author riding polo
pony Blueberry

widely known. I was elected to the presidency of the Rotary Club and became a Paul Harris Fellow.

After several years, the Rotary Club decided to conduct a fall-only polo match, which left the spring dates open. Realizing the magnitude of community support and enjoyment of equestrian activity, I initiated the Equus Ventures: Equestrian Exposition. This encompassed a polo match, jumping for cash competition, carriage driving, horse racing, and a demonstration of fox hunting with hounds.

Some of the hard-working and creative Equus Ventures executive committee included:

The author riding his favorite thoroughbred, Dynamite

Polly McCune provided accounting and artwork supervision.

James Edward Alexander, an attorney and author, and served as coordinator.

Eddie Maple, Hall of Fame jockey served as the equine advisor and discipline organizer.

Willie Dunne served as disciplines organizer and was in charge of equipment.

Teri Namba and **Charlie Gibbes** were honorary board members (deceased).

Following the positive launch of the Equus Ventures Expo, I was invited to join the Lowcountry Hunt. Mounted, live fox hunting was steeped in tradition— red jackets, politeness, and terminology. Through the generosity of landowners, the Lowcountry Hunt is privileged to ride on and provide stewardship for private plantations. Galloping with the hounds at full cry through pristine terrain was most exhilarating and memorable.

The pleasure of riding with the hounds and taking multiple jumps is not without peril. Safety and good manners are of foremost concern.

The most beneficial effect I derived from working with horses is the therapeutic psychological well-being imparted. Working with horses helped foster trust. One specific psychological symptom that decreased was my hypervigilance—referring back to my need to carry a weapon since returning from Nam. The horse, being an animal of prey, is also hypervigilant. Walking toward the horse in a nonthreatening manner gives it an opportunity to accept an approach. I still own two thoroughbreds with which I have fox hunted. At my age, my riding is pleasurable but not nearly as robust as in my younger years. My equestrian lifestyle has been with me for more than five decades.

Ben Tucker

Soon after Carmel and I moved to Savannah, we were invited to a cocktail party attended by some interesting community leaders, including Ben and Gloria Tucker. Upon being introduced, I asked Ben if he was The Ben Tucker, who wrote "Coming Home Baby." Our conversations led to a lasting friendship since we had several musical acquaintances from the New York jazz scene in common.

My children always enjoyed listening to Mr. Ben perform as they grew up. On one occasion, Linda, my current wife, and I took our daughter Emily, then six years old, to Ben's club, Hard Hearted Hannah's. Emily gave Ben a big hug, and he invited her onto the bandstand. Before we knew what was happening, the band played a rousing rendition of "Happy Birthday." Emily

Internationally known bassist Ben Tucker and his wife Gloria with the author

thoroughly enjoyed being in the spotlight, waving to the audience. We thanked Ben, explaining that it was not her birthday, but she loved the applause and attention. Our children grew up enjoying the affection Mr. Ben showed them.

Ben performed with many of the top jazz musicians of the day, including Billy Taylor, Peggy Lee, and Herbie Mann, to name a few. Ben also became involved in the music publishing business. Among the many tunes he published, "Sunny" was his greatest success and firmly ensconced among contemporary standards.

Aside from being a legendary jazz musician, Ben was a community role model noted for integrity and friendship. He purchased the WSOK radio station in Savannah and used his influence to benefit the community in countless ways.

Unfortunately, Ben Tucker was killed on June 4, 2013, after enjoying the game he loved. A speeding car hit his golf cart. Ben will be fondly remembered by all who knew him.

Lou Rosanova

After I decided to move south in 1974, I learned that the Teamsters Union Pension Fund owned the Savannah Inn and Country Club. My father was a lifelong member of Local 560 of the International Teamsters Union, serving as a shop steward at the Trans-American Freight Corporation.

An acquaintance of my father's, Mr. Anthony Provenzano, gave me his business card introducing me to Mr. Lou Rosanova, the general manager of the country club. I called and asked to speak with him, mentioning that he and my father had some mutual business friends. I gave Mr. Provenzano's card to Lou

The author with Lou Rosanova in Italy

Rosanova, and without hesitation, he said, "Doc, I've got to do whatever you say." From that point on, Lou and I had a great relationship until his death, 40 years later. He referred countless dental patients to my practice, and we enjoyed many good times together. He often called me "figlio mio," meaning "my son" in Italian.

Lou frequently visited Carmel and me for dinner at our home on Wilmington Island. One time my oldest daughter was helping to prepare the hors d'oeuvres, when Lou said, "Honey, be careful with that knife." Lou, being such a large, gravelly voiced man, was very intimidating, and Rebecca began to whimper. Lou said, "Honey, I'm sorry," in his gruff voice, and Rebecca responded, "No, you ain't!"

On one occasion, Lou and I met for breakfast at the Kings Bay Country Club in South Florida. A very big, unattractive man, Chuckie O'Brien, joined us. He was introduced as Jimmy Hoffa's stepson (as in the Teamsters Union). In his classic manner, Lou said, "I like to stand next to Chuckie because he makes me look like Gregory Peck" (the dapper Hollywood actor). Lou was a man larger than life.

Lucky Thompson

Lucky Thompson, a fine saxophonist, who played with Count Basie, Duke Ellington, Dinah Washington, and other jazz luminaries, was planning to move to Savannah in 1979. Ben introduced me to Lucky since Lucky was having great difficulty playing his saxes and flute because of his poor dental health. I restored his teeth, and we became friends. Prior to coming to Savannah, Lucky was a professor of jazz studies at Dartmouth University, but he disliked the politics and moved south. At this time in my dental career, I worked in my Hilton Head satellite office one day a week, and Lucky would accompany me. We had great conversations about life and music in general. I loaned him the office car so he could spend the day walking on the beach enjoying nature and "communicating" with the seagulls. He would return to the office and pick me up at 5 p.m.

One day I received a call from a patient, Garry Moore, a TV personality, who was a jazz lover. Garry had heard that Lucky was in the area and wanted to meet him. We got together on several occasions at Garry and Betsy Moore's home in Sea Pines. I thoroughly enjoyed listening to the dialogue recounting Lucky's musical experience.

My two older daughters, Rebecca and Kristen, would often accompany me to dinner with Lucky. He was fond of writing letters and wrote two regarding his perception of my daughters' characters. He was a true artist.

I provided Lucky with a rent-free apartment in a building I owned in historic Savannah. He managed the property since I was gone most of the day. Lucky circulated and talked to various people, but he began to feel that they were secretly observing him. He also felt that someone was digging under his apartment even though he lived on the ground floor. In cold weather, he thought that the hissing of the radiator was emitting poison gases to kill him.

Since I was in contact with Lucky, Clark College in Atlanta called me. They wanted to honor him by having a Lucky Thompson Day at their annual jazz festival, but he declined, stating that his was a God-given talent, and by accepting money, he would "prostitute" himself.

Finally, it was determined that Lucky was a paranoid schizophrenic. He was a danger to himself and could no longer function as a member of society. His brother-in-law, Archie Moore, an actor and boxer, facilitated moving Lucky to the West Coast, where he died in 2005.

Despite his illness, Lucky was a trustworthy man of exceptional talent. He recorded several albums under his own name and played as a sideman on many others.

6

THE DARK AGES

I maintained a busy professional life and didn't realize that I had returned home from Vietnam a complex emotional person. Sometimes I would cry, and other times I hid behind a wall I had built. I didn't realize that I was mentally unbalanced. To me, hypervigilance was normal, and I rarely left home without a weapon.

Being a Vietnam veteran was not favorably looked upon by many people in our society. Upon discharge, we were instructed not to put information about our return in the local papers for fear of retribution against our families or us.

Professionally, I was working hard and doing well despite the dark clouds hidden in the recesses of my mind. Sometimes I would get extremely emotional at the slightest provocation.

Divorce and Living Downtown

I was working late hours, and my struggle with PTSD was eroding my home life. During this time, Carmel and I had two children: Rebecca, born in 1974, and Kristen, born in 1976. Despite family support, I continued sliding into severe dysfunction. Work became an obsession and totally consumed me.

I chose to do the unthinkable:

I separated from my beautiful family.

I moved into a two-room unfurnished apartment in one of two buildings I owned at 216–218 Abercorn Street in the historic district of Savannah, Georgia. I leased a table, a bed, and a sofa. That was all. My friends called it "The Cave" and said I was reverting to Vietnam. I passed their comments off as a joke, but it was the truth.

As my earnings increased, I began to buy more rental properties in the historic district, but I still lived in "The Cave," where I felt protected. I carried a weapon 100 percent of the time and lived this lifestyle for many years.

The Dark Ages

The following story is connected to my reversion to life in Vietnam:

On April 8, 1971, I lost two friends, Thomas Lee Sonderman and Matt John Wodarczyk, who were Military Intelligence chopper pilots. They had lived adjacent to me in Vietnam and provided transportation wherever I had to go. We spent a lot of time talking about family back home and buying new cars upon our return to the world. They enjoyed listening to performances by The Real Thing. They said they were so "short" they could "fall off a nickel," meaning their tours would soon be over in May 1971.

Tom Sonderman was a single guy from Derby, Kansas. He was 22 years old and spoke enthusiastically about the Datsun 240Z that he had ordered.

Matt "Woody" Wodarczyk was 28 years old and married with two children. He was a quiet family guy anxious to get home to Philadelphia, Pennsylvania.

Men make plans, and God laughs. They took off from Bien Hoa on a routine mission, and it was suspected that their ship was hit by an RPG (rocket-propelled grenade), only about a mile from the base.

The following are poems referencing my PTSD:

Woody, Tom, and Me

You know, I spent tonight alone, talking with
Woody and Tom;
It's been nine years almost to the day since they've gone.
They said they didn't mean to leave, but that's the
way things go.
And they told me not to forget them, nor Jim...
nor Joe.
I can remember packing their stuff to send back to
their folks;
Just some clothes, old letters and pictures we took as jokes.
There were those photos that hung by their beds,
Tom had one of his sports car; Woody's were of his
wife and kids.
Funny how two country boys and a city guy developed
such friendship ties.
We laughingly made a pact that we'd not forget those
times till the day we died.
After living through hell together,
We figured there wasn't a storm in life we couldn't
weather.
Well maybe they got the easy way out, or perhaps
fate let me slide.
I guess it'll be a while before I know for sure
But there have been many nights I've sat up and cried.
I know you're in a hurry so I'll end the quickest
way I can...
You see, Woody and Tom are two of my buddies,
that were killed in Vietnam. —Written in 1980

Solitude of a Birthday

Sitting alone on the night of my birthday,
I remember this very time ten years past,
by the way.
Things were a lot different, yet in many ways
the same.
Then, like now, there were neither candles nor cake.
No old friends were around with jokes to make.
Of all my family, none were on hand.
Today I'm back alone in the world…
ten years ago, I was in Vietnam.
—Written May 10, 1980

Why?

I don't know the answers or why
I've gone this way.
My thoughts return to Nam
night and day.
It's been rough drifting through a marriage
with two loving daughters,
Not being able to explain why I can't
be their daddy like I ought to.
I'll just continue to stalk through
life,
and on the surface, I'll play the game,
it's the best way I know to hide the
hurt and pain.
I've built a wall around me that gets
tougher every day,
But I came home from Nam with no
wounds
so, I'm really okay.
—Written in 1981

I found the following poem in a magazine memorializing the 25th anniversary of World War II. It has remained with me all these years, and I thought it would be appropriate to include in reference to Vietnam.

Letter to Saint Peter
By Elma Dean
1944

Let them in, Peter, they are very tired;
  Give them couches where angels sleep.
  Let them wake, whole again, to new dawns
  fired.
  With sun, not war. And may their peace
  be deep.
  Remember where the broken bodies lie.
  And give them many things they like.
  Let them make noise.
  God knows how young they were to have
  died.
  Give them swing bands, not gold harps,
  for these are boys.
  Let them love, Peter— they had no time—
  Girls sweet as meadow winds
  with flowing hair.
  They should have trees, bird songs, hills to
  climb,
  Tastes of summer and ripened pear.
  Tell them how they are missed; say not to
  fear.
  It is going to be alright with us down here.

A Letter from Home

The following commentary is an excerpt from a letter I wrote to my good friend, now deceased, Sandy Gellein, who saved all my letters until his death. These letters contained my interpretation of factual information taken from my tour of duty in South Vietnam.

"Please note the sometimes unusual mindset of jumping from mentioning 'the fragging' of sleeping troops and then easily discussing ordering stereo equipment or cameras to send home.

There was no emotion in the way I lived in Nam. A wall was built to keep feelings out of the picture. Perhaps this compartmentalization contributed to delayed PTSD.

Another example of this incongruent mindset is noted when we were placed on RED alert to prepare for 'sappers' coming through our perimeter wire and then casually writing about ordering a new car for my return home.

I tried to make the best of it, never fearing injury or death."

7
MY LIFE TODAY

Linda

Mrs. Mary Lampman came to my office for a dental appointment. She mentioned that her daughter, Linda, had always enjoyed riding horses in Saudi Arabia, where her father worked for ARAMCO. When Linda came in for her appointment, we discussed our love of horses, and I invited her to become acquainted with my polo ponies. She was pursuing her master's degree in nursing education, and I was proceeding with my divorce.

Linda was an excellent horsewoman and "saddle-pal." After several visits, Linda expressed her interest in riding my best horse, Bogey. He was a very responsive, small thoroughbred. If you even thought about making a turn, he would complete a 180-degree change of direction in a heartbeat. Unfortunately, he threw Linda and she broke her right arm and pelvis in three places. I felt terrible. She spent two weeks in St. Joseph's Hospital and several months healing.

Our relationship grew stronger, and I jokingly said during our courtship: "In order to avoid a lawsuit, I have to marry Linda." We were married in November 1983 in Savannah. Both Rebecca and Kristen were in attendance, which made our day complete. We shared hours riding together and initiated multiple charitable equestrian events for the community. After 36 years, we are still happily married.

Linda and I lived at the Landings on Skidaway Island prior to moving to our current home in Rose Hill Plantation. This was a far cry from living in downtown Savannah in my tiny "cave."

Realizing that the equestrian lifestyle was important to us, we purchased a five-acre lot affording us privacy, stabling, access to riding trails, and the polo field. Fortuitously, we built a large house to accommodate family and friends.

Emily, our youngest daughter, was born in 1989. She attended school in Savannah while Linda pursued her neonatal nursing career at Memorial Medical Center. Handling the logistics of getting Emily to school was made possible by my in-laws, Mary and Al Lampman, both deceased, who lived in Savannah. My schedule was arranged as needed to facilitate transportation to extracurricular activities. Emily spent her high school years at Hilton Head Preparatory School, which kept us in South Carolina.

Joseph and Rosemarie Carpitano

My interest in guitars and treating dental patients led to a long-time friendship with Joseph and Rosemarie Carpitano. We both owned D'Angelico guitars and arranged to meet and discuss our rare instruments while enjoying a delicious meal prepared by Rosemarie.

Joe and I had a mutual love of classic Italian songs as well as selections from The Great American Songbook. Our musical compatibility, fueled by Rosemarie's excellent culinary skills, led to a friendship lasting more than 15 years until Joe's passing.

Conversations ranging from our Sicilian Heritage to growing up in Brooklyn were most enjoyable. Many informative and humorous anecdotes were interspersed in our conversations. Only someone growing up in that golden era could appreciate the fullness of living in that epicenter. Rosemarie graduated from Brooklyn College as did I. She went on to earn her master's degree and became a school principal. Joe was a successful

Guitarist and friend, Joseph Carpitano, playing a 1938 New Yorker D'Angelico guitar and the author playing a 1959 New Yorker

businessman, and he established the St. James Paper Company.

Our friendship grew as we traveled together to the North Carolina mountains and Italy as well. Those days of friendship, music, and good food will never be forgotten and will always be cherished.

Mom

Aside from taking care of our family growing up, Mom enjoyed a business career working for Metropolitan Life Insurance Corporation. After Dad passed away, Mom realized she was limited in her independence due to the fact that she never learned how to drive a car. It was not common for women to drive during their formative years. However, at the age of 65, she decided to learn.

At this time, Mom was living with my brother, Nolan, and his wife, Jean, in Flemington, New Jersey. To gain experience, she limited herself to driving country roads. In the years after my father's death, I would occasionally fly up to New Jersey to visit the family. Travel was scheduled so that I could fly back with my mother, and she could enjoy an extended stay with Linda, Emily, and me.

I never can forget my mother's reluctance when I mentioned she would have to drive my pickup truck. I told her it was either drive the truck or ride a horse. (Of course, I told her this in jest.)

To make her feel more comfortable, I purchased a 1974 Ford Brougham Limited, which she drove during her extended time with us. It was known around town as an emerald green tank, and the kids were embarrassed to be seen in it. They affectionately called it, "The Bomb."

Once, I purchased two plane tickets for Mom and my Aunt Jean Modica to visit me in Savannah. Aunt Jean was unable to come. That left me with one unused roundtrip ticket that I thought my elderly mom could use at another time. I booked her a flight using Aunt Jean's ticket, and my mother became increasingly apprehensive about using a ticket that was not in her name. This was in the 1980s, so travel was much more relaxed.

I had a friend working for the airlines who assured me that we could get my mother past security in a wheelchair with an outdated driver's license. Everything went smoothly, and Mom used the ticket successfully. She asked me how I arranged it, and I told her that I explained to the ticket agent that my mother was mentally ill and could not speak well. That's what got her through. My mom couldn't believe that I told the airline staff she was crazy. But we were successful in using the ticket.

Mom had never been to Italy, so I arranged for her and Emily to join a group trip we were taking. One of our side excursions was to the small island of Procida, near Capri. We arrived by boat and then took a taxi to the Palazzo d'Avalos, a castle and former prison, located above the town. It was an interesting and exhilarating panorama. We then decided to walk down to the docks and have lunch. Once we got to the marina, we realized that Mom was nowhere to be found. I immediately retraced our steps and discovered that she was enjoying taking part in a wedding reception with the local residents. They had welcomed the American woman who was fluent in the Italian language. Mom was oblivious to the fact that we had a time scheduled to return to the mainland. This trip to Italy was an unforgettable high point in her life.

My Family Today

Considering all of my 76 years, I have been most fortunate to have a loving, beautiful family.

At the young age of 22, I married Carmel, and we had two daughters, Rebecca and Kristen. Reflecting back on some difficult times, I cannot imagine the state of my mind and sadness caused by my mental problems. God had a plan for our family, and I am thankful for that.

In 1990, Carmel moved to New Jersey so the children could be closer to our families. Rebecca and Kristen received an excellent upbringing surrounded by love during their formative years. I cannot thank Carmel enough for such an excellent job of bringing up our daughters.

The author with his grandchildren

Rebecca graduated from Muhlenberg College in Allentown, Pennsylvania, and married Christopher Hayevy, a Villanova graduate. Rebecca began working in the Financial Services Industry for Pershing LLC immediately after graduating college and was there for 16 years. While at Pershing she earned multiple securities industry licenses and worked her way up to the vice president level. Rebecca is currently part of a successful Wealth Management Team at Merrill Lynch. Chris is in internal audit in the insurance industry. She and Chris have two daughters, Sophia, born in 2003, and Sarah, born in 2006. Both granddaughters are engaged in various sports and are part of the high school chorus. Travel is an important part of their lives and they are fortunate to have visited Japan, several countries in Europe, Canada, Mexico, and many spots in the United States. Linda and I went on a River Cruise in Europe with Rebecca and her family in 2018.

Kristen graduated from Villanova University with a double major in English and Secondary Education and a minor in History. She married Peter Singagliese, also a Villanova graduate. She proceeded to earn a master's degree in Education, taught English, and then started her family. Natalie was born in 2005, followed by Michael in 2007, and Daniel in 2010. The grandkids have their individual personalities and participate in multiple after-school activities involving sports, music, and theatre. Kristen decided to devote the majority of her time to raising her children while Pete pursued his career in finance. Kristen returned to teaching in 2016. The logistics of scheduling school and extracurricular activities is a monumental but workable task. Dixie, their dog, is an integral part of the family, providing an immeasurable amount of love and pleasure to all.

After graduating from Hilton Head Prep, Emily attended the University of South Carolina in Columbia. She switched majors and received a bachelor's degree in interdisciplinary special education with a minor in psychology from Liberty University. She began her teaching career as an applied behavior therapist working with special needs children for a school district in Lexington, South Carolina. After several years and a divorce, Emily was offered and accepted a job teaching kindergarten and integrated special needs children at St. Gregory The Great Elementary School only two miles from our Bluffton residence. Linda and I welcomed our daughter moving back into our spacious home, especially since we have a private apartment wing. I was reminded that our youngest daughter was now 30 years old.

Our household is brightened by the presence of Remington, the family dog. I still have two thoroughbred horses, and interacting with them has been part of my salvation. After returning from Vietnam in 1971, I was diagnosed with PTSD. Despite receiving various psychological and neurological treatments, I found that equine therapy provided me with very positive results.

Other significant components of my life at this time are renewing my proficiency as a guitarist. Music has been a great part of my life and is truly a universal language. I also enjoy shooting skeet and sporting clays as a way of maintaining reflexes and improving eye-hand coordination. Above all, I am thankful for our families' health and good life.

As we age, DON'T LET THE OLD MAN IN.

8

MEMORABLE PEOPLE AND SIGNIFICANT AWARDS

Throughout my 76 years, I have been blessed by several individuals who have significantly impacted my life. In addition, I have received several awards. I'm humbled by these awards and grateful for these personal relationships and friendships. I feel they deserve to be recognized in their own chapter.

Dr. Frank Frates

Dr. Frank Frates, also known as "the Coach," was the iconic symbol of the University of Medicine and Dentistry, New Jersey. As a retired naval captain, he insisted on excellence and shaped the lives of those he touched. Unlike other health professionals, the Coach made sure that we wore clean, crisp trousers and clinic jackets, and spotless white shoes.

He enforced the principle: "If you can't get something right the first time, when will you have the time to do it again?" Our dental class started with 59 students but graduated 32 with DMD degrees. This attests to the fact that the price of being the best carries significant responsibility. The Coach inspired many people. I am proud to have been a FTM (Frates Trained Man).

General James Hollingsworth

I met General James Hollingsworth at the Officers' Club in Fort Jackson, South Carolina in 1969. He enjoyed my guitar playing when I sat in with the band. Many nights we would close the club. The general and I would talk about benefiting our country most by serving in Vietnam. I enlisted quietly, and I got our affairs in order. In about 10 weeks, I left for Nam, as did the general.

After a couple months of settling down in-country, he contacted me at my base camp, Cu Chi, and arranged to pick me up in his Huey (UH-1 helicopter). We planned to have dinner and headed for Saigon, however a message was received that a recon patrol had made contact with a VC battalion in the area. General Hollingsworth instructed the pilots to get closer and the door gunners opened up with two M-60 machine guns. General Hollingsworth enjoyed a good fight, and he exhausted his ammo. Reinforcements arrived, and we then proceeded to Saigon for a "leisurely dinner."

I chose to include my unique acquaintance with General Hollingsworth due to his positive influence on my life.

The following is quoted from *Ambush:*

"He was a general officer playing Davy Crockett in the Vietnam War. Being one of the Army's characters, he never let anyone forget it. In spite of his Texas cow country drawl, war fighters cotton to him. He plays at the game of war as if he has no hope of getting out of this life alive" (Marshall 1969, 152-159).

Brigadier General Hollingsworth did not let rank stand in the way he evaluated a man. His fairness and courage have impressed me to this day.

Captain Vic Aliffi

One of the most memorable people I met while serving with the 1st Cavalry in Vietnam was Jay Victor "Vic" Aliffi. It was a very hot day in Bien Hoa when Vic's unit came through our perimeter after spending a couple days in "Injun Country," which is what the Cav called everything outside our perimeter. He looked like a bandit: he had crisscross bandoliers of ammunition draped over his big frame, and he carried a sawed-off shotgun.

Vic earned a reputation as a tough, no-nonsense soldier. He was awarded a battlefield commission to captain, two Silver Stars, eight Bronze Stars, a combat Infantry man's badge, and multiple other decorations. His military citations repeat the lines: "with complete disregard for his own safety." He was responsible for saving several lives and silencing the enemy.

After our initial meeting in Bien Hoa, Vic and I became fast friends, and I learned about his family in Savannah, Georgia. I invited him to some of our social activities, carefully chosen because Vic was a remarkable soldier with an impeccable career. I wanted to protect him from some of my escapades.

Vic wanted to be a career soldier, but despite his excellent combat record, he was discharged since the army no longer had a place for brave combat soldiers. Having completed his college degree, Vic attempted teaching and coaching sports. He also became an automobile salesman. I attempted to help Vic acclimate to civilian life since it turned out to be so different than that of a war fighter. He left the army in 1976 on a medical discharge. Vic Aliffi died of a brain tumor on May 18, 2002. I regret not having spent more time with Vic in his final years.

Dr. Herbert Bartlestone

Under Dr. Herbert Bartlestone's guidance, I learned a great deal.

I enjoyed working under the tutelage of such a unique man. Following are words that describe this mentor in the dental profession:

He possessed unrelenting standards of excellence.

He was a gifted teacher and an idealist.

His ideas will provide the basis for the inspiration of colleagues for years to come.

Dr. Herbert J. Bartlestone shaped my life in a very positive manner. He died suddenly in 1973.

Bronze Star Medal

The Bronze Star Medal was awarded for "meritorious achievement in ground operations against hostile forces in the Republic of Vietnam."

I volunteered to go on missions that were beyond my job description. My positive interface with fellow soldiers was likely a contributing factor.

In addition to the Bronze Star, I received the following:

The author being awarded the Bronze Star Medal in South Vietnam

Vietnam Civic Action Honor Medal, Meritorious Unit Citation, Vietnam Service Medal, Vietnam Campaign Medal with 60 device, and National Defense Service Medal.

THE UNITED STATES OF AMERICA

TO ALL WHO SHALL SEE THESE PRESENTS, GREETING:

THIS IS TO CERTIFY THAT
THE PRESIDENT OF THE UNITED STATES OF AMERICA
AUTHORIZED BY EXECUTIVE ORDER, 24 AUGUST 1962
HAS AWARDED

THE BRONZE STAR MEDAL

TO

CAPTAIN SANDY S. TERMOTTO, 053-36-5292, DENTAL CORPS
UNITED STATES ARMY

FOR

MERITORIOUS ACHIEVEMENT
IN GROUND OPERATIONS AGAINST HOSTILE FORCES

IN THE REPUBLIC OF VIETNAM - JULY 1970 TO JUNE 1971
GIVEN UNDER MY HAND IN THE CITY OF WASHINGTON
THIS 20th DAY OF MAY 1971

CREIGHTON W. ABRAMS
General, United States Army
Commanding

SECRETARY OF THE ARMY

Carnegie Hero Fund

Established on April 15, 1904 by Andrew Carnegie, the Carnegie Hero Fund Commission recognizes outstanding acts of selfless heroism performed within the United States and Canada. The Carnegie Medal for Heroism is given "not for the glory of the individual, but that descendants may know and be proud of their heritage."

I was awarded the Carnegie Medal for Heroism for my actions

Carnegie Hero Fund Commission

Pittsburgh, Pennsylvania

This certifies that

Sandy S. Termotto

has been awarded a Carnegie Medal
in recognition of an outstanding act of heroism:

Bronze Medal awarded to Sandy S. Termotto, who rescued Albert L. Tolle from burning, Bluffton, S.C., February 6, 1979. Tolle, aged 20, was unconscious and pinned in the front seat of an automobile that had been involved in a collision and on which the engine was afire, the flames spreading into the front compartment. Termotto, aged 34, dentist, forced open the passenger door, knelt on the floor, and managed to free Tolle. He then pulled Tolle out of the automobile, which a short time later was engulfed by flames. Tolle recovered from burns he had sustained.

_____
President

_____
Manager

on February 6, 1979.

On that Tuesday, I was driving back to Savannah after working on Hilton Head at my satellite office when I came upon a horrendous scene. Several cars had been involved in a head-on collision. Two people died, and a third man, Albert Lee Tolle, age 20, was unconscious and pinned in the front seat of one of the automobiles involved.

Bystanders were yelling to get away from the car and that the unconscious man was dead. I attempted to free Tolle to no avail, but I then saw his hand move. I was not going to let this person die. Despite my jacket being singed by the intensifying flames, I grabbed part of a bumper and wedged the passenger door open. I knelt on the floor and managed to free Tolle. I then pulled him out of the car just before the car exploded into flames. He recovered from the injuries and burns he sustained.

I never saw Albert Lee Tolle again, but I did receive a thank-you from his mother.

The Key to Savannah

In 1980, I was awarded the "Key to the City of Savannah," which is presented to citizens who demonstrate outstanding humanitarianism and citizenship. I received this key specifically for charitable fundraisers and for being awarded the Carnegie Medal for Heroism.

EPILOGUE

I have written about my experiences, reflecting on the trials and tribulations of my life. Not one life, but a blend of six lives...growing up in Brooklyn, my musical life, military life, professional life, equestrian life, and the present.

This was all written from my perspective, including the occasional bumps and curves in the road.

GLOSSARY

ARC-Lite: high altitude B-52 bombing missions along Cambodian border

Bird: any aircraft

Booney Hat: soft camouflage hat

Bunker Bunnies: Red Cross workers who would have sex with GIs for money

Bush: area outside of base camp

Charlie: Viet Cong

Chuck: reference to Viet Cong (VC)

Chu Hoi: VC who wanted to join the American cause

Class 1 Yard: all food passed through this point of entry; where veterinarians checked the food

Co Diep: pretty girl

Concertina: a roll of tangled barbed wire

Contact: engaging the enemy

Cowboys: bad gooks on motor scooters who would ride next to you in traffic and quickly grab your camera, watch, etc. and escape into traffic

DEROS: date eligible to leave Nam and return to the world

Deuce and a half: a two and a half ton truck

Diddy-Boppin: jive walking and talking

Didi mau: run fast

Dinks or Gooks: derogatory name for Vietnamese

Donut Dollies: Red Cross nurses

Dust Off: medical evacuation by helicopter

"Em Joe": brother or mister (an expression of respect)

Fatigues: green or combat-color uniforms

Firefight: exchange of small arms shooting

Fire Support Base: a temporary artillery base to support ground operations

FNG or Fanug: Fucking New Guy

Fugazi: crazy or screwed up

Get a Shot of Leg: to have sex

Getting Short: very little time left in-country

Grunt: infantryman

Gunship: a helicopter armed with various weapons

Hooch: living quarters in base camp made from discarded plywood, screen, Styrofoam, etc.

Hooch Maid: young Vietnamese maid

In-Country: to be in Vietnam

Injun (Indian) Country: Jungle territory outside base camp perimeter

Kit Carson Scouts: VC that switched sides were made to walk point and warn us of any traps

Klick: kilometer

Lamb Fucker: slang for a veterinarian

Lifer: career soldier

Loach: LOH-1; a light observation and recon helicopter

Lurps: long-range reconnaissance patrols

Mamma San: an older Vietnamese woman who oversaw hooch maids

Med Caps: going into villages to provide medical/dental care, i.e. civic actions

Mike-Forces: montagnards trained by U.S. Special Forces (SF)

Montagnards: also known as "Yards," mountain people in

Central Highland not linked to or liked by Vietnamese; family-oriented, excellent, courageous fighters

MOS: military job description

N.V.A.: North Vietnamese Army

Nui Ba Den: Black Virgin Mountain

Number 10: #10 is bad (the worst), #1 is good (the best); mainly used with Vietnamese as slang in reference to rating the looks of soldiers

Papa-San: an older Vietnamese man

Pastry Pigs: unattractive Red Cross workers

Peacenik: anti-war demonstrator

Puff the Magic Dragon/"Spooky": large fixed wing fully armed aircraft (DC-3 or C-47)

R&R: rest and relaxation/recreation

Rack: bed

Re-Up: reenlist

Sapper: enemy soldier carrying satchel charges attempting to breach our perimeter

Sin Loie: "So sorry," sarcastically, i.e. "Sorry Charlie"

Slick: a UH-1 helicopter used to carry troops, also known as a Huey

SOG: Special Operations Group

Stand Down: return to base camp for a short rest; don't engage

Steel Pot: helmet

TET: Vietnamese New Year

The Iron Triangle: the land between the confluence of the Saigon River on the west and the Hinh River on the east, bordering Route 13, "Ambush Alley," about 25 miles north of

Saigon; a very strategic area

Thumper: an M-79 grenade launcher

Tunnel Rats: small U.S. soldiers often with only a pistol and flashlight who flushed out the VC from their underground hide-outs

Uncle Ho: Communist leader Ho Chi Minh

White Mice: South Vietnamese police who wore white helmets, gloves and short-sleeve white shirts

Willie Pete: white phosphorus rockets or grenades that could pierce any known armor; also used to mark targets

Zapped: killed

BIBLIOGRAPHY

S.L.A. Marshall. 1969. *Ambush*. Cowles Book Company, Inc.

INDEX LISTING

McCune, Polly
Modica, Lou
Modica, Marietta
Modica, Onofrio
Moore, Garry
Mystics, The
Namba, Teri
O'Brien, Chuckie
Passions, The
Perlis, Al
Pizzarelli, Bucky
Quinones, Colonel
Roe, Bill
Rosanova, Lou
Russo, Frankie
Russo, Joey
Russo, Joseph
Russo, Nolan
Russo, Phillip
Russo, Rose
Ruth, Bill
Santa, Ed MAJ
Scherrer, General "Pony"
Shealy, Dave
Sinatra, Thomas Dr.
Singagliese, Kristen
Sonderman, Thomas Lee
Spence, Catherine
Stahle, Bill LTC

Termotto, Arthur
Termotto, Caterina
Termotto, Emily
Termotto, Linda
Termotto, Martha
Termotto, Nolan
Termotto, Saverio
Termotto Gallo, Carmel
Thompson, Lucky
Trafficante, Family
Tucker, Ben
Valenti, Joe "Tampa Joe Beans"
Wayne, Chuck
Welton, Iva
Whipple, General Sim
Wilson, Colonel Harry
Wodarczyk, Matt John "Woody"
Yarrow, Peter

PLACES:
12th Evacuation Hospital
216-218 Abercorn Street, "The Cave"
ARAMCO
Bensonhurst
Bien Hoa
Black Virgin Mountain "Nui Ba Den"
Brookdale Hospital
Brooklyn College
Coney Island

Country House
Cu Chi
Dau Taeng
Flemington, New Jersey
Fort Jackson
Fort Sam Houston
Fort Hamilton
Hard Hearted Hannah's
Hilton Head Island, SC
Hilton Head Plantation
Honey Horn Plantation
Hong Kong
Liberty University
Long Binh
MacDill Army Airfield
Maimonides Hospital
Memorial Medical Center
Micali Terrace
Modica Bakery
Muhlenberg College
New Utrecht High School
Palmetto Dunes
Phouc Vinh
Procida
Rose Hill Plantation
Saigon
Savannah, GA
Skidaway Island
Staten Island

Tan Son Nhut
Tay Ninh
The Iron Triangle
Ton Sonhut
Trang Bang
University of Medicine and Dentistry of New Jersey
Villanova University